Brief Moments In A Lifetime

by
F. A. Balint

Cork Hill Press
Carmel

Other books by F.A. Balint

The Poetry of New Hampshire
ISBN 1-930648-42-1

CORK HILL PRESS™

Cork Hill Press
597 Industrial Drive, Suite 110
Carmel, IN 46032-4207
1-866-688-BOOK
www.corkhillpress.com

Trade Paperback Edition: 1-59408-246-4

Printed in the United States of America

-"Our jeep had just crested an unnamed peak in the Rif Mountains of Spanish Morocco, when suddenly armed guerrillas leaped out of the brush and surrounded the vehicle.

They were Berber tribesmen ominously attired in native turbans, djellabas and dark tunics, while across their chests were crossed bandoleers, fully loaded. An eerie silence ensued."

-Rasheed's Guerrillas

-"It has been written that during July's Encierro (Running-of-the-Bulls), the entire male population of Pamplona is comprised of psychopaths and/or masochists. We three Americans did nothing to harm their reputation. It was the moment of truth!"

-Running the Bulls

-To understand my life, one must savor the rhythm of the "Vagabond's Song." It's a timeless, discordant melody that only dreamer's hear. A gypsy rhapsody that makes one drift and roam to the ends of the earth, as in a vagrants dream.

-Wanderlust

To my Granddaughter Alyssa,

"May you find a kinder, gentler world."

Grandpa Frank

The following narrative, comprised of short stories, reveals the travels, observations and events that shaped the world of F.A. Balint.

Tales of adventure, humor and unfolding history that surrounded him as his vocation carried him across the United States, then to Europe and Africa. Share the magnificence of soaring mountains, the Sahara, ageless cathedrals, and Roman ruins while exploring the vagaries of Man.

Civil War, Berber tribesmen, astronauts, scientists, thieves and foreign legionnaires all were his travel companions.

His post marks included Oued Zem, Ronco, High Lonesome, Casablanca, Tangiers and Cape Canaveral.

A life in pursuit of Man's ultimate "raison d'etre."

INDEX

FOR THOSE WHO ASK WHY

Next time I will walk more quietly, speak more softly, and ask more questions. Next time I will attempt to master one of life's most difficult challenges, I will "learn to listen." Family and friends will be the forefront of concern, bees and butterflies will hold a position of admiration, and enemies will vanish, as I will create them no more. Next time I will pick more wildflowers.

We humans pick a mate to walk with, to confide in, and to love. We are the only species with the ability to reason, to select a deity and pursue our private interests. In effect, we alone have the ability to select a role in virtually all of our endeavors except health, and even there, we influence it.

A lifetime is a wonderful odyssey, a series of exploits of which some are happy while others are tinged with sadness, tragedy or misfortune. We receive them all as life's cards are dealt. It begins with sublime innocence and then come the formative years coupled with outside influences but if one is fortunate, learning will become the driving force. What an intoxicating experience the trek elicits. A myriad of possibilities engulfed in a maze of endless opportunities provided the individual wisely selects the appropriate path—a difficult task. The signposts are there however we must select carefully. There are books, people and teachers to assist but beware of those who deal in deceit and chicanery.

In the following stories I have attempted to sketch some of the more memorable moments that occurred during my walk through life. These stories emphasize my zest for travel and education. The events vary in scope and breadth; one spanning decades to arrive at the final conclusion, while another consumed a total of five seconds.

I am a wealthy man, not in monetary wealth, but in a satisfied, contented existence of one who has achieved most of his goals. I have stood on launching pads, sat in boardrooms, and walked lonely beaches seeking answers. Many times however, I believe the answer bore hollow echoes, for the search is the essence of the journey.

From the coal-dust-laden streets of Ronco, Pa. to the Champs Elysees, it has been an exhilarating quest. Now, with a wonderful friend and wife at my side, I am truly experiencing the full harvest of my passage. The twilight shadows have now appeared and a surreal tranquillity has enveloped my being with the realization that I have maneuvered the journey, and now I am at peace. This tranquillity did not come easily, as the path was laden with difficulties and many personal deficiencies had to be overcome.

Growing up in Ronco, where social activities were scarce, I learned that to read a book transcended boredom and freed one's mind to awe inspiring exploration. Thus my lifelong romance with literature was born, and I was never alone again. To read a book is to absorb the heart and mind of another. I am continually enthralled by reading autobiographies and biographies. Those who lived wrote them, loved and learned.

Thus I have fulfilled my desire to leave a record of events I encountered, leaving them for others to scan and ponder. It creates a patchwork quilt of my passing. Far too many individuals become disciples of hatred, bigotry or racism while others succumb to desires of avarice, but knowledge should always be the quest. For it is an educated mind that can maneuver the pitfalls and quagmires necessary to insure a life of quiet satisfaction. Education does not guarantee wealth or health, but instead is a guiding influence that enables an individual to wrestle with adversity and not become a victim of it. Education does not require formal schooling instead it can be fulfilled with observation, reading and, above all, the ability to listen.

In 1998 I completed my autobiography, a three-year undertaking. The book is unabashedly my story, warts and all. There are regrets, of course, mistakes are integral to every journey. My intent was the exposure of the story, including personal trials. Everyone encounters difficulties but the measure of the individual is the recourse taken. Let me trust that my performance was satisfactory

My passage has been blessed with good health. I have endured 67 years without a broken bone and an absence of a serious malady until recently, when I was diagnosed with Parkinson's Disease. Am I despondent, hell no, I've traveled a long way from Ronco. If ever walked a man who is satisfied with his passage, it is I!

Dare to live and do the improbable: travel, change jobs, read books, take that other fork in the road, and above all- do not become a twenty-five year employee. Tell them to stuff their gold watch. Do not reach the latter stretch of life with those two words strung around your neck like an albatross- "What If?"

Life is a divine happenstance, be it created or accidental, but what a glorious occasion it is. If your life has been fulfilled, I ask you, have you ever heard a coyote's howl or the bugle of an elk? Have you paused and observed the marvel of a hummingbird in flight or watched an eagle soar aloft on golden wings? What about at night, have you seen a meteor's trail, tried to capture a comet's hair, or witnessed the ever changing panorama of the aurora borealis? To live is to enjoy every nuance of life's passage, to become totally absorbed with one's existence.

Next time pause to watch a baby cry. Observe the sublime innocence of one who's mind has yet to be corrupted by an adult, stop to enjoy the sight of a violet blooming in a forest glen, or read a passage of poetry. Your inner being will thank you and ask, "What took you so long?"

LIFE'S TREASURES

Scenic visions are everywhere
From mountains that scrape the sky,
To shoreless seas and oceans
But we, we walk on by.

Endless plains awash with flowers
With bouquet to make an angel cry,
Yet, we see and tarry not
For we, we walk on by.

Dew clad forests
With sunrises that bring a sigh,
But we pause not
As we, we walk on by.

Nature's beauty surrounds all
Yet, we turn not an eye
For we are too much in us
As we, we walk on by.

(continued)

We, who have been granted witness
Pause not to dignify,
Life's special blessings
As we, we walk on by.

I shall ponder these truths
'Til death, and ask why,
We took it all for granted
As we, we walked on by.

F.A. Balint

A COAL MINER'S STRIFE
RONCO, PA. 1934-48

Suddenly the mine whistle sounded, forlorn and ominous. All activity in Ronco ceased immediately as the evil portent echoed throughout the "Patch." The sound emanated from the mine tipple, that structure that rose over the mine shaft which swallowed and disgorged coal miners daily. The sounding indicated an accident, someone was injured or dead! The town's reaction to the whistle was always the same, paralysis.

Dad worked in the mine and in 1941, brother Bob entered its employment. The Balint family resided in house #151 and it was there, in 1934, that I entered the world. The family was now complete, three boys and one girl.

The whistle and reaction were an accepted way of life in the "Patch," as the small mining settlements in Pennsylvania's bituminous coal fields were labeled. The presence of coal was the sole reason these patches existed. They were built by the Coal Companies to house and isolate their employees and in doing so, the employer gained even greater control over the hapless immigrants. The plan succeeded beyond expectations.

The Patches were all constructed similarly and generally housed approximately 200 souls. The streets were dirt comprised of coal dust residue and streetlights were nonexistent. The houses were duplex in construction, consisting of four rooms per side-two upper and two that were at ground level for each family. All dwellings had an outhouse and an open space of approximately 50x25 yards between the two structures. This area was primarily used for a vegetable garden or a play area for children. However, the most identifiable trademark of all patches was the pallor of smoke and coal dust accompanied with the odorous smell of sulfur that constantly hovered over the region.

The miners had come from mainly Eastern European countries that were devastated by world war one. Usually the men arrived alone, penniless with few skills and very little education. World War I, the "War to End All Wars" had just ended, leaving misery and poverty in its wake. Eastern Europe had been especially devastated and many countries now possessed new geographical boundaries, thus the desperation of the moment made many people uneasy and ready to flee. They came from Czechoslovakia, Yugoslavia, Hungary, the Caucasus and the Carpathian Mountain Regions to take one of the most undesirable jobs in America-that of a coal miner! Incredibly, for most of these men, it offered an opportunity for a better future. They took the jobs that no one else wanted a job that was hard and dangerous—and performed underground. My father was one of these men.

Little publicity was given to the fact that agents of the wealthy Coal Barons recruited these men in Europe. Their resume was a reputation as reliable, hard workers. Once the men agreed to the offers, their visas were stamped with destination-the coal region of Southwestern Pennsylvania. Dad's visa indicated Uniontown, Pa.

Most of these men arrived alone, as Dad did. After passing through the ritual at Ellis Island, they were sent to their final destinations. There they lived, worked, married, raised families and died. Very few ever revisited their homeland. Many, like Dad, worked 30 plus years in the dark dank coal tunnels, constantly under dangerous conditions, until their lungs were black, inside and out. The equivalent of 10 years in darkness!

Hardships for these men were compounded by language. Even though the immigrants spoke four or five languages, none spoke English—the language of management. Therefore, quite often, it was necessary to use an intermediary to complete an exchange of information, or to obtain a service—sometimes with disastrous results.

It soon was common practice for the parents to have their children read all correspondence written in English, and even write letters when required. Local officials recognized this problem and classes were held for adults but attendance was very poor and soon the program was discontinued.

During World War II, my brothers were in the Air Force and my sister had married, therefore I wrote all personal correspondence for the Balint family. It made a ten-year-old boy very proud to contribute.

Coal mining was indeed a very dangerous endeavor, and safety was low on all priority lists. The Ronco Mine was known as a "wet mine" This meant that the overhead leaked water as the mine tunnel followed the coal vein as it meandered under the Monongahela River. Rats became one of the miner's best friends and safety alarms. The men actually fed the rodents from their meager lunches, because they knew that rats could sense danger, a tremor that could result in a cave-in or the deadly silent killer-methane gas. Thus when the rats left an area so did the miners.

Labor strikes were rampant throughout the coalfields, thus increasing the schism between labor and management. The treacherous working conditions coupled with increasing demands of the Coal Barons resulted in a seething cauldron of unrest. The Coal Magnates knew that if they could keep the "Patches" isolated, they could control the miners. This continued until a fiery Welshman named John Llewellyn Lewis, an unruly union organizer who quoted the bible and Shakespeare equally well, arrived on the scene. Unions were needed to force improved working conditions and continued to be necessary until greed and corruption permeated the labor establishment in the 1950s. When John L Lewis stepped down from the UMW Presidency, Tony Boyle, whose avarice was unquenchable, succeeded him. Tony Boyle later died in prison for the murder of J. Jablonski, a rival union leader.

But as dangerous and dirty as coal mining was, it was the housewife who lived in oblivion. It was an aspect of the miner's family life that was totally overlooked. Her existence personified the lost soul. Alone, alienated from other women, except the next door neighbor, these women were totally absorbed in the daily drudgery of existence. The plight of other women in neighboring towns was unknown, as methods of communication were nonexistent. Rearing the children, cooking, washing, ironing and cleaning in an atmosphere of coal dust were all they knew. The women were not happy and thoughts of leaving Ronco were fantasies. Entertainment consisted of a three-mile hike, every two months, to see a movie in Masontown as Dad never owned an auto or learned to drive. All housework was done by hand, even the making of soap and clothing, with the pall of the dreaded mine whistle portending disaster always looming overhead.

Pictures of three men were often prominently displayed in many homes. These were photos not taken but found in discarded magazines or papers brought home from the local grade school by children. These men were a symbol of hope. The three were Franklin Roosevelt, Jesus Christ and John L Lewis. The arrangement of the pictures on the wall was the inhabitant's choice, and quite often, John L. Lewis was on top.

A GATHERING
Ronco, Pa. 1945

The scene was solemn and foreboding. It was enveloped by an aura of tension-a gathering of forlorn forgotten men that in desperation, clung together for survival. They were a clan, a byproduct of the great American depression, who had withdrawn from the race.

These men were overwhelmed by the economic upheaval that had transpired during the period of 1929-34. Jobs were lost, families decimated and all personal feelings concerning pride, ambition and honor destroyed leaving but a hollow human shell, whose only goal was daily existence. Thus, these "Hobos," as they were labeled, fled into a life of oblivion, abandoning home, family and friends with the only transportation available-the train. These shadow men stole aboard trains from coast to coast leaving behind a legacy put into song and book.

The date was January 3, 1945, the dead of winter. The time was 10 PM, quite past the bedtime for an eleven-year-old boy, but fueled by curiosity, I sat on top of the slate heap created by the H.C. Frick Coal Mine in Ronco, Pa. I was perched approximately 400 feet above the scene and nearly 100 yards distant. Below me, oblivious to my presence, lingered a vagabond cast in disarray, the railroad track, and 50 yards further, the dark icey waters of the Monongahela River.

Adjacent to the railroad track sat a steel drum, from which a blazing fire emanated and attempted to fend off the cold dank air, while casting an eerie halo of light that penetrated the darkness. In the shadows of this surreal ritual, fleetingly appeared the silent figures of four individuals clad in torn coats, overalls and pull-down caps, lowered to eye level. The cold night air gave credence to their breath, but not to their voice. It was a séance of despairing souls that constantly changed its cast as shadows crept into the halo of light only to periodically fade away. Subject of their attention was the fiery drum offering warmth, while perched on top sat a steaming caldron, brewing a hobo's repast.

Gossip among Ronco's inhabitants had alerted me to the existence of these wayward travelers. They seemed to materialize spontaneously then vanish with the next train, pausing only for a short respite. These figures, cloaked with a veil of mystery appeared to be ragtag residents of the night, whose solitary daily quest was survival. Their hopes were drained, and apparently aspirations and dreams were beyond comprehension and attainment.

In the years that followed, I would occasionally reflect upon these scenes that I witnessed on several occasions, at the same location, but always with a different cast. I wondered what fate finally delivered to these wayfarers, and I always secretly wished them well. It is a poignant memory that has remained with me through the years, and I always wondered about the finality of their journey. Future authors and songwriters attempted to glorify their passage, but as an observer of these rites, I witnessed only a closed door to a life beyond.

Perhaps I, too, belong to an outcast clan of individuals, whose existence is but a search for answers we hope to never find. An answer provides closure, while questions provide an ongoing search, and therein lies the quest. A journey to always seek and ponder the ultimate "Why"?

THE "MAN"
BOSSIER CITY, LOUISIANA-1954

Dynamite oftentimes does indeed come in small packages. When a guy stands five feet-five inches tall and weighs approximately 155 lb. and is the biggest man in the joint, he's either a hellva man, or the place is crowded with pygmies. In the personage of Joe F., the former was the case.

Joe was a bouncer de-luxe, a man whose presence often riled and infuriated patrons, instead of calming them. The fact is, six feet men awash in booze do not tolerate criticism or advice from a man who's six inches shorter. Yet Joe was a master of tense situations, and being a former prizefighter, a challenger for the title, he usually carried the day.

My presence in Louisiana, compliments of the US Air Force, was due to my scheme of putting in for a transfer during the first week of a new assignment and it was working perfectly. This scheme was consistent with my desire to travel as much as possible. I was now at my fourth location in less than one year. The time was 1954 when I met Joe, the pride of Cajun Country. I had been transferred from Virginia to Barksdale AFB, near Bossier City, La., and as a Fuel Analyst I was assigned to the Petroleum-Oil-Lubricants tank farm. Joe worked there as a civilian employee.

I had recently graduated from a school in New Jersey, conducted by a consortium of oil companies, to provide the Air Force with competent fuel analysts for the burgeoning missile programs, both military and civilian endeavors.

He was an amiable soft-spoken fellow who was in his middle forties. Our personalities meshed, which was a surprise considering our diverse backgrounds, and this was before I learned that Joe was once a prizefighter who fought for the crown. Guys on the tank farm often commented on the speed of his fists. Once I said that I'd like to see him fight, "Hell," one GI retorted, "Go to the BC Bar in Bossier City, Joe is the bouncer there." So that Saturday off I went. I'd heard about the place; it was rumored to be the liveliest joint around, lots of chicks.

What I witnessed that night was unbelievable. There was Joe. One of the smallest guys in the joint trying to pacify arguments before fighting broke out. Only the patrons who were familiar with Joe respected him. They had either seen him in action or personally learned the hard way, as most of the new rowdies did. Joe spoke with a soft voice, but his fists spoke loud crescendos.

Joe considered himself a gentleman and never struck any troublemaker in the face. Being a prizefighter, he knew anatomy and could floor just about anybody with body blows. "I don't have to mess up a man's face," he often stated, "unless they're two at one time. Then its no holds barred, it's me against them." That night I saw two altercations that required Joe to "put a man down." The speed of Joe's fists was unbelievable, and his feet were those of a dancer. The action was impossible to describe as it occurred very fast and ended in seconds. Not once did either rowdy lay a hand on Joe.

The next day at work, I was telling all that would listen about what happened at the BC Bar but they just smiled; they had been there. Joe and I became fast friends, which surprised a lot of people as Joe was a quiet individual who didn't mix socially. Soon we were referred to as the Cajun and the Yankee, the "Odd Couple." Then one day he asked me to spend a weekend at his home in the Bayou, which I readily accepted. When others heard the news, they grinned broadly and told me, "Frank, you ain't seen nothing yet."

In Louisiana, the descendants of the French exiles from Arcadia are known as Cajuns. The people were expelled from Nova Scotia during the eighteenth century. Cajuns have many outstanding qualities, but one of their superior traits is friendship; it lasts a lifetime. Through the years, Cajuns picked up another nickname, "Coonass." The term is slang and not denigrating.

Joe and I traveled about twenty miles to reach his home. We passed through a vastly different landscape than I'd ever seen before. We were in Bayou country, surrounded by swamps and moss laden cypress trees. Joe's home was located at water's edge under a gnarled, old cypress tree, with nary a neighbor's house in sight. The house itself had a run-down, shabby appearance, as the heavy moisture of the area was especially harsh on wooden structures.

Joe's family, consisting of wife Marguerite, and two small sons, were very friendly. Supper would not be ready for an hour, so Joe proposed a boat ride. I readily accepted, as the bayou was a place of mystery for me, and I wanted to explore as much as possible. I had spoken to Joe in great lengths concerning my love of the forest and my experiences while trapping and hunting, so he was keenly aware of my interests. We clambered aboard his fourteen-footer, equipped with a ten-hp Evinrude motor, but Joe reached for the oars immediately and passed one to me. "The motor is for emergencies," he explained, "too noisy, and it scares every critter in the bayou." So off we went into a truly eerie world. It was broad daylight, but the sunlight never seemed to penetrate the bayou. There was a gloomy, surreal atmosphere that was almost foreboding.

We rowed in silence, with Joe identifying various snakes, turtles and other critters. The bayou is an incredible microcosm of nature. Snakes were everywhere, hanging from trees, on stumps and swimming nearby. Several times Joe cautioned me concerning low hanging limbs ahead, as they contained snakes drooping downward. It then dawned on me that for the first time in my life, I was in an area that contained all four poisonous snakes indigenous to the United States. Copperheads, rattlers, coral and water moccasins all lived in the bayou. The thought did not elicit elation within me.

The mosquitoes and other insects were now swarming around us in clouds so Joe passed a can of repellent that I generously applied. We traveled for about twenty minutes when Joe asked me if I could find the way back to his house. Yes, I replied, somewhat hesitantly. I was confident that my outdoor instincts, honed in Pennsylvania's back wood, would prevail, but I soon confessed that I was out of my element. Joe laughed, "Don't feel bad, you're lost, but this is a different environment than you're used to. Water has no trails or paths and landmarks are difficult." He was right, I had never seen a hostile environment like the bayou offered. Nature seemed to have developed a malevolent nature, and closed around us.

He then lit a lantern and gingerly hung it on a pole in the bow of the craft. As the light emanated, dozens of glowing orbs returned the light, as the eyes of many creatures were upon us. Occasionally, we heard large splashing sounds, to which Joe calmly replied, "Gators-probably." I was Joe's first Yankee visitor to the bayou, and he was enjoying my apprehension

The next day we toured the bayou. It was Joe's world and he enjoyed it. We fished in the afternoon and caught many fish, mainly bass. We kept ten fish, all over a foot long. I asked Joe what was the limit and he replied matter-of-factly, "In the bayou, its what the boat can hold-who's gonna argue." He then informed me that we were attending a dance that evening, as he had the job of "peacemaker." He called it a "Bayou Ball," but later I found out he may have said, "Bayou Brawl."

That evening we "decked-out in our finest Sunday-go-meeting outfits." This included our cleanest blue jeans and sweatshirts; then we were off for the festive occasion, about three miles distant. We left after dark in Joe's boat via lantern light. Gads, what a spooky trip; again there were many "eyes" watching us with reflected light. It was now obvious that the vast amount of traveling in the bayou occurred by water. Sounds of the bayou were everywhere, as the area was alive with activity. Finally, through the trees, lights appeared and as we approached, I observed a very unusual setting.

The dance floor was a wooden deck, supported by pilings, and surrounded on three sides by water. The remaining side abutted an island where crude bleachers supported numerous trashcans filled with beer and booze. Around the outer periphery of the deck, a wire was strung from which lanterns were hung. It was apparent that a hellva party was already in progress. Music was blaring, people were dancing, hooting, yelling-and hell- most of the crowd was already drunk. One thing was certain, a lively evening lay ahead. Joe beached the boat and someone yelled out, "Be good boys, the bouncer has arrived."

The first thing Joe did was introducing me to the crowd, very loudly. He said I was a Yankee (which sent shivers down my spine) and I was a friend, and if anyone had a problem with that, they had to deal with Joe. The evening fulfilled my wildest expectations, and some I never dreamed existed. There was swearing and cursing, accompanied by a lot of jumping and stomping that I privately named the "Bayou Turkey-Trot." The musicians impressed me; I had never experienced their equal as fiddlers. They poked, strummed, picked and made their fiddles do everything but dance. Joe described the music as "Authentic Down-

Country Bayou Coonass Music." The dancing and festivities continued in full swing until a loud splash was heard. Then all activity stopped as someone had danced off the deck into the water. It happened twice that evening and created a panic as men grabbed poles and flashlights to rescue the wet dancer. Treating a snakebite or worse is not advisable by lantern light with drunken attendants.

There were only two fights that evening, as Joe said later, "A quiet evening." The first, Joe dispensed very quickly, as a six-foot Cajun went down very fast. The second brawl commenced when two men jumped Joe from behind and placed him at a severe disadvantage. The two drunks, both larger men, had him down, "wrassling around" on the deck. But soon, Joe righted himself, and I witnessed why a prizefighter's fists are legally defined as "lethal weapons." Joe was clearly agitated at being bushwhacked, and the first guy caught an uppercut and went "splash" over the side. The second opponent went down on the deck in a heap very quickly. In all, Joe threw about ten punches, but most were a blur.

Ninety percent of the crowd was very fond of Joe. He was a local hero who nearly made it to the top; he brought the Cajuns respect and they were proud.

The evening ended on a peaceful note as twenty, twenty-five boats departed into the insect and snake infested darkness. It was an eerie parade through the bayou; drunken men steering their boats, as no one used a motor, into the blackened abyss. By lantern light they went and I surmised an accident had to occur, but I was wrong.

One of the last boats to leave, Joe and I finally set out into the bayou and I turned to watch a sight I would never again witness. The eerie lanterns and torches appeared to be a rite of the damned or sorcerer's sacrifice-perhaps a tribute to Druids. Gradually, the lights faded and disappeared among the gnarled moss-laden trees. I queried Joe about previous dances, did anyone ever have an accident? His response was hesitant, but he replied "once." He said that on that occasion, after a party an old friend named Philippe, a bachelor and loner disappeared. During the ensuing days, he was missed at his usual haunts. Concern mounted, tensions increased, and a search was mounted among the local gentry. About thirty boats scoured the area for two days; finally his boat was located-drifting aimlessly- and then the badly decomposed body of Philippe was found. The bayou and its denizens had done their job. Philippe's remains were buried on one of the few high spots in the bayou. The authorities were never notified, as Cajuns took care of their own. Its amazing that in this enclave called America, such diverse cultures exist, but again, isn't that what it's all about?

CULTURE SHOCK
SHREVEPORT, LA. 1954

It was to be Shreveport's finest hour. The city fathers had proclaimed a renaissance. The time had arrived for Shreveport to obtain the prominence it deserved and assume its position as an enlightened bastion of the arts and entertainment. One that would provide its citizenry accesses to classical music and the theater, a dawn of a new era. Now the descendants of the CSA and the DAR would have access to the same cultural offerings as the rest of the nation. And what more splendid example than classical music, even more enhanced by the rich tenor voice of the world-renowned Metropolitan Opera Star, Jan Peerce.

For the Civic Leaders of Shreveport, it was time to prove H.L. Mencken; Editor, Author and Critic, who compared the existence of Southern culture "to the vacuum of interstellar space" in his critical essay "The Sahara of Bozart" wrong. Their position maintained that the South was indeed the home of cultural refinement.

A series of six concerts were planned for the summer of 1954. The city fathers sponsored and promoted the program, with the local newspapers enthusiastically touting the coming events. They were to include musical and theatrical presentations, and the final commitments with the artists were being finalized.

I had been assigned to Barksdale AFB, near Bossier City-a suburb of Shreveport-during the summer of 1954 when the announcements appeared in the local newspapers. Posters were scattered throughout the city and surrounding suburbs "ballyhooing" the great revival.

I followed the news of the upcoming events very diligently and secretly bought a ticket. Around the squadron, and especially in the Day Room, the idea of classical music and operatic arias were severely derided, and caustic epithets were constantly hurled against anyone who supported them. In the jargon of the GIs, only a complete "NUT" would spend $20 for a ticket to hear some music sung in a foreign language. When I privately informed my best friend Jerry that I bought a ticket, he stared at me in disbelief. Jerry was a homegrown Indiana farm boy, very laid back and as goodhearted as they come, but music was not his forte. He couldn't distinguish "Dueling Banjos" from "Swan Lake." Then he asked, very seriously, "Has the gasoline fumes at the tank farm scrambled your brains." Now Jerry was my best friend, so I decided not to tell anyone else. He laughed, "Only you-he roared, by the way," he continued, "are you a pecan or a walnut?" Then he added insult to injury, "You know that I can blackmail you, so never cross me or I'll spill the beans."

I had never witnessed an operatic performance, but I recalled my introduction to classical music in high school when I played clarinet in the first chair of the woodwind section for a large musical assemblage. The occasion involved my being selected to participate in the Fayette County Symphonic Orchestra, and I found it to be an exhilarating experience. When questioned about enjoying a vocalist singing in a foreign language I couldn't translate, my response has always been the same. "It's like hearing a violin or horn being played by a great virtuoso, the talent and music are one."

As the momentous day was nearing, newspaper advertising increased. Glowing reports of surging ticket sales urged the populace to "buy now" and especially "come early" as parking might be a problem. Reading the reports puzzled me as the concert was being held in the cavernous auditorium which held approximately 10,000 avid country-music fans every weekend for the wildly popular "Louisiana Hayride."

The comments uttered in the Day Room made me seethe inside and I exacted revenge on the pool table. I was rated the number one pool player in the squadron, but now I elevated my game to a higher level. I now not only wanted to win but quite often I would "run the table" without my opponent ever getting a shot during the game of "eight-ball." None-the-less, the caustic comments continued unabated.

Finally, the day of reckoning arrived, and that evening I left for town alone. Jerry held his silence, therefore my transgression had not been exposed. I exited the base akin to Benedict Arnold sneaking off into the night. I arrived at the auditorium and was surprised, as parking didn't appear a problem. The local dignitaries were present en masse, and I observed the large "Welcoming Banners" for Jan Peerce fluttering overhead as I entered the building. Locating my seat, I was ecstatic that it was very close to the stage, then looked around and surmised that I misunderstood the curtain time as a very small crowd was in attendance. I then observed that everyone had a seat near the stage; a strange foreboding sensation suddenly grasped me-something was amiss.

The hour arrived, the lights dimmed, and Mr. Peerce walked on stage. He was given the loudest standing ovation that an audience of approximately 500 could muster. He then graciously acknowledged the reception and sang the opening aria, "Nessum Dorma."

Upon the conclusion, and amid a scattering of applause, he smiled with affable understanding, walked to the front of the stage and addressed the embarrassed audience. He asked for a request. With the awareness of everyone present, that the cultural event was a disaster of epic proportions, it was compounded and dealt the final death knell when a plaintive voice replied, "Mr. Peerce,...do you know, Home on the Range?"

The audience shuddered and shrank low in an attempt to disappear in their seats. Mr. Peerce replied by stepping back, and graciously sang a rendition. The curtain was then lowered, and the Shreveport Cultural Revolution quietly and peacefully expired.

Perhaps the ghost of H.L. Mencken was seated in the loge for as I left, I pondered that perhaps old, acerbic H.L. was right in his assessment!

A VOYAGE THROUH HELL
A NOR'EASTER-NORTH ATLANTIC,
JANUARY-1955

It was the personification of terror and evil. Boiling, hissing foam spewing forth from the gates of Hell in torrents mountain high, then crashing down on our frail vessel. Never had I experienced terror of this magnitude before, I was watching my worst nightmare. Then it dawned on me, what I was witnessing was the first day after the storm when we passengers were allowed to go on deck. What the hell was it like the five previous days?

It was January 19th, 1955, and 3000 Air Force and Army personnel, all certified landlubbers, had just set sail for Casablanca, French Morocco aboard a Liberty troopship. The Liberty Class of ships, built by Kaiser-Fraiser for the US Merchant Marine during World War II, was constructed with a round keel instead of a sharp one. The design, theoretically, offered fewer tendencies to capsize and provided greater buoyancy in rough weather but guaranteed a much rougher ride. This voyage was indeed one to remember.

Slowly the ship churned out to sea, and, by nightfall, North America was a memory and before us lay eleven days of the perils that the North Atlantic Ocean had to offer. I had gone below deck only briefly to locate my bunk and position my duffel bag nearby. It was located on "D-Deck." The bunks were stacked six high, with two feet of space between them-we were packed like sardines. One look and I vowed to spend as much time as possible "topside."

The first "survival" bulletin came over the intercom several hours after departure. They explained, apparently with dead seriousness, that in case of an emergency, each deck would wait patiently as the upper decks evacuated. The implication was "D-Deck" would mark time until approximately 2,000 men on decks "C, B and A" went topside, before we progressed upwards "in an orderly fashion." During this polite interlude, mind you, the damn ship is sinking-now let us examine the intelligence of that announcement for a microsecond, before we puke. There naturally would be immediate and total chaos, hell-any fool knew that, and those below "A" deck were goners.

The first night I slept poorly. Hardly anyone slept, as card games were in constant session. Everyone had money, as we were paid prior to departing Ft. Dix, thus poker was in session constantly, and by flashlight after "lights-out." My plans included no seasickness! I would eat only two meals a day and greasy stuff, such as bacon and sausage were taboo. Alas, Mother Nature's plans trumped mine.

I went on deck the second day and noticed that the swells were larger and getting choppy. Also the sea was no longer blue-green but turning a dark gray. I ate very little; I had survived day one, now for day two. I played a little cards in the after noon, and slowly the day passed into oblivion.

Day three dawned with ominous, portentous overtones. The ship was rolling heavily, and many more men were seasick. I headed topside, but I was stopped. "It's off- limits" a crew member advised me, "We're bracing for a Nor'easter." The proclamation sent shivers through my spine. I had read many frightening novels concerning Nor'easters, and now fate placed me directly in one's path.

What damn idiot authorized the ship to leave port with 3000 landlubbers on board with a storm bearing down. Did weather forecasting become extinct? The rolling of the ship became more pronounced as the day passed. Seasickness now reached epidemic proportions. Card games ceased to exist, and the lines in the mess were very short, but eating was not on my agenda as my stomach was sending queasy signals. I returned to my bunk and accepted that day three was a disaster, and unknown to me, there would be a few more.

Day four to eight were pure hell. Two storms were raging, one outside the ship, and the other within. No one was eating, and thus the dry-heaves set in. I lay in agony. At night, I prayed the ship would sink, who cared…at least we would all be at peace. Night intermingled with day, gloom abounded throughout the vessel. I existed in a quasi-world of light and darkness, punctuated by the ship's crashing between, what must have been, gigantic waves. The ship's rolling increased until, finally, I knew we would sink. I marveled at the grand design, very clever. Seasickness was created to keep one's mind in a state of torment, and therefore the ship's peril would be ignored.

Day five was beyond hope. The sanitary conditions of our deck were deplorable. The ship was rolling severely, and shipmates were puking everywhere, as some men made it to the latrine, but most didn't even try. The moans and groans increased, until the sound of regurgitation reverberated through the deck. Even the seasoned seamen were affected, as the deck was slippery with liquids and undigested food. Occasionally I arose and visited the mess hall to attempt to eat as I was starving, but the little food I ate appeared later on "D-Deck."

Most of the men remained in their bunks, but with trepidation. With the bunks stacked six high and filled with sick men who couldn't "make it" to the latrine, it was not recommended to "hang over" the side lest you get "drenched." Leaving the bunk therefore was done post haste.

Finally, day eight arrived. I was weak but physically improved, thus I visited the mess. I nibbled on dry cereal and then noticed that the main deck was not off-limits. Even though the sea was extremely frightening I stayed on deck till nightfall. It was better then being entombed within the bowels of this semi-upright vessel.

Gradually activity aboard ship returned to normal, as sanitary conditions improved. With out need of orders, groups of men banded together and swabbed the decks. Soon poker games reappeared, and dice could be heard rolling to someone's vocal challenges. Even the lines in the mess were growing longer. That night I actually slept, due mainly to exhaustion.

On day nine, the ship was now in a more southerly location, and I enjoyed basking in the sun the entire day. The highlight of the day occurred in the afternoon when, off the starboard bow, I espied the first whales I'd ever seen. They were lumbering, giant mammals swimming leisurely together.

Day ten required everyone to attend informational briefing concerning French Morocco, its inhabitants and customs. Emphasis was placed on the Muslim religion and its traits; i.e. never point a camera at a Moslem woman as the camera was regarded as the "evil eye." Then a serious briefing was held concerning venereal disease and condemning sexual encounters, as diseases have been encountered for which cures were unknown.

That last night aboard ship stirred the poet within my soul. I was leaning on the rail staring into nothingness, the ship rising and falling on gentle swells, when I saw it. I gulped and swallowed very hard, was it delirium or was I just imagining it? Off the port side, slightly astern, I saw lights. They were dim, as a haze covered the water, but they were there. Impossible, "We were two ships passing in the night." I had read that passage a zillion time in literature, but to view it was an elixir beyond comprehension. "Who were they I wondered, and what was their destination?" I savored every minute of the scene lest it never pass my way again. I stared long into the darkness, after the lights faded into the distance, trying to imagine one more glimpse. A few minutes later, looking skyward, I spied the constellation "Southern Cross" another first observation for me. I stared at it for ten minutes realizing that we were indeed approaching the Southern Hemisphere. I realized that the Azores were somewhere near at hand so I closed the voyage remembering Joaquin Miller's poem:

"Behind him lay the gray Azores
Behind the Gates of Hercules,
Before him not the ghost of shores
Before him only shoreless seas."

RASHEED'S GUERRILLAS
THE RIF MOUNTAINS
SPANISH MOROCCO-1955

Our jeep was in low gear as we crested the top of an unnamed peak in the Rif Mountains of Spanish Morocco. George and I were in full dress uniform; plus we had two American flags mounted on the front fenders. The road was gravel and narrow, thus speed was not advisable, when suddenly it happened. From both sides of the road, armed guerrillas leaped out of the brush and surrounded the vehicle. I stopped immediately, and George and I exchanged glances. Everything became very quiet as no one spoke.

From their physical proportions, I realized that they were Berber tribesmen, much more robust then the average Moroccan. They numbered about twelve and all wore turbans, djellabas and dark tunics, while their chests were crossed with bandoleers, fully loaded. All were armed with rifles and carried knives at their waist; they were a formidable group, and with full facial hair, very menacing.

Then slowly and solemnly they pressed closer, when one Berber, obviously the leader, broke into a big grin and shouted "Amerikan." Suddenly all the Berbers became animated and smiled. I spoke in French and the leader, Rasheed responded, as the tension had been broke

The Berbers were the first inhabitants of Morocco. Their presence extended back thousands of years to the Neolithic Era. They are fierce, proud combatants who, during World War II, aided German General Rommel and his Afrika Corps, in their occupation of North Africa. It was the Berbers who eventually fought the Foreign Legion to a standstill and greatly assisted in the liberation of Morocco.

The stoppage by Rasheed and his men was brief. He asked if we had any American cigarettes. I offered my pack, almost full, to Rasheed and George, bless his hide, broke open a carton he had stashed under his seat and passed them around. Rasheed then asked if we saw any French patrols on the road. I replied negative, and he waved us on, but warned us "to be aware of the crooked Frenchmen and Jews in Tangiers."

The city of Tangiers is located at the northwestern tip of Africa. In the early 1950's, Tangiers was the center of an enclave of territory that functioned as an International Zone, under the control of multinational entities. Its claim for notoriety embraced questionable financial institutions, permissive drug laws and prostitution. In Tangiers, the value of currency fluctuated widely on a daily basis. I observed, in the local French newspapers, that many 25% fluctuations occurred in a single day, quite appealing to a

GI who only made $100-$200 a month. It was the possible profitable financial transactions that appealed to me.

Thus I organized a legitimate trip to visit Tangiers and exchange money; however some aspects of the enterprise might be classified as a little shady. My scheme involved Sgt. George M. who, as a very street-savvy ex-gang member of Roxbury, a suburb of Boston, could handle himself in a tight situation-which the trip turned out to be.

What I needed to negotiate a successful venture was greenbacks. All GIs had their greenbacks replaced by Military Script, which bore a great resemblance to monopoly money, immediately upon arrival on foreign soil. It was military policy. When word circulated that George and I were going to Tangiers on a "money run" we were inundated with script from members of our squadron. In two days I had 5 grand in my possession. Thus my first task was to convert the script into greenbacks which I readily accomplished-paying a commission to local Arab black marketers-whom I easily met with on the base. Nouasseur AFB was a huge depot, enclosing many square miles, which was guarded by Arab Nationals per an agreement negotiated by the U.S. State Department (another questionable governmental policy). In effect, the Moroccans had free access to the base, while American sentries guarded selected areas within.

The one problem that perplexed me was where in the hell would I hide the money during the trip, as I was certain that we would be stopped in route. A ragtop military jeep, which was the only vehicle I had access to, was wide open for prying searchers. Then an idea struck me. I would hide it in the most visible location on the jeep, in one of the 10-gallon jerry cans that every military jeep carried, perched on the rear of the jeep.

My plan was simple. I would place the money in several reddish-brown plastic bags, once I knew the amount of money involved hence the size of the bags. Then I would add enough water to cover the bags, after which I would fill the can with gasoline. My rationale being, the gasoline would float on top of the water and not dissolve the plastic bags. Also, it would smell like gas and the dark red color of gasoline would aid in preventing the moneybags from being seen if anyone peered in. To remove the bags was simple; an ordinary coat hangar would suffice.

The night before our departure, George and I were quietly sipping beers at the NCO Club, when I brought up the subject of the hiding place for the money. George had never queried me on the subject; which was puzzling to me. He laughed and said, "Don't tell me until we're under way, I've got a good reason for not wanting to know the secret." He then added, "Frank, you know I can't hold my booze-hell three beers and I'm shot. Therefore, if don't know, I can't spill the beans." I said "OK George" and laughed. George was well known for "going out for a night" with thirty cents in his pockets as draft beer at the club was only ten-cents a glass. Some nights, he bragged, he carried fifty-cents but that was when he wanted to "show off" and treat others. Thus George was unaware of the hiding place until we were under way, and when informed, thought it was a novel idea.

Friday morning at 5 a.m. we left Nouasseur with two 48-hour passes in our pockets, and two huge lumps in our throats. The distance to Tangiers was approximately 230 miles, an easy one-day round trip. The excursion was all business, sightseeing was left for another day. The motor pool, which provided the jeep, was in on the deal, thus we had the best jeep on base.

We progressed smoothly though French Morocco, but as we were about to exit we were halted by American Military Police. They flagged us down, and a Tech Sgt. approached the vehicle in the usual surly manner. After taking our papers he slowly circled the jeep, examining every nook and cranny. During his inspection, he touched both rear gas cans, as they protruded out behind the vehicle. George smirked at his actions, and shortly we received permission to go on to Tangiers.

We entered the sprawling city and were greeted by a cacophony of horns, merchants yelling, a Muezzin calling the faithful to prayers, and traffic, mainly bicycles. I scanned the skyline of the city of 130,000 inhabitants looking for tall buildings, which usually denoted the business district. Soon afterwards we located two banks.

We decided to do two transactions, less conspicuous. I went first, and George guarded the jeep, as Arabs were notorious for pilfering. Everything went smooth, and soon George was in the other bank doing his transaction. Both tellers were somewhat leery, but our military uniforms allayed their fears. We made a killing, the boys at Nouasseur would be ecstatic, as we received 450 francs per dollar versus 325 per dollar in Casablanca.

The trip back was uneventful, exactly what we wanted; we didn't encounter Rasheed and "his band of merrymen," but descending the mountainous area I understood why Rasheed wasn't around. After turning a bend in the road we encountered a patrol of Legionnaires who stopped us and very cordially queried us. The Sgt. was French, which surprised me, as I was aware that ninety percent of the legionnaires were German, who didn't or couldn't return to their homeland for various reasons. I explained that we were returning from Tangiers, which surprised him, but I offered no information about our encounter with Rasheed, as I informed George later, because Rasheed treated us OK and George agreed.

The conversation with the Sgt. was in French which George didn't understand-a fact that baffled me. Classes in the French language were held three evenings a week at Nouasseur and I attended as many as possible, but ninety-five per cent of the GIs never attended.

Upon arriving at the base, we were greeted like conquering heroes and immediately queried about the "next" trip. In the ensuing week I was notified that I was being transferred to the port of Casablanca, therefore, if there were to be a future trip, it would be soon.

Two weeks later, amid clamoring from other GIs, George and I planned another trip. Gathering money and exchanging it for greenbacks did not pose a problem. In addition, Hosi M., a Sgt. of Spanish descent, asked to accompany us. George and I discussed the matter and agreed that another body, who spoke Spanish, could be a valuable asset.

We set out early and passed unmolested through French Morocco, encountering minimal traffic. Soon we entered the Rif Mountains and upon cresting the same peak as before, we were surrounded by Rasheed and his guerrillas. A deadly silence greeted us for several seconds so I shouted "Bonjour, Rasheed." He grinned and responded "Francois, is that you?" Although he appeared friendly his guerrillas kept back and appeared ill at ease. The group surrounding us now numbered about thirty and was brandishing more modern automatic weapons.

George broke out the cigarettes and we passed them around. Meanwhile, Hosi was fuming. "You bastards," he swore, "you knew this would happen but didn't warn me." "Cool it, just a little indoctrination," commented George. We passed out four cartons of cigarettes and then Rasheed got very serious. "On your last trip," he asked, "did you see any Legionnaires in the area?" I knew I was being tested and I knew he was aware of what happened that day so I spoke truthfully; "Yes, we encountered a group of Legionnaires, about fifty. We gave them no information about meeting you or your men as you treated us cordially." Rasheed stood about two feet from me during this interrogation with his coal black eyes boring into me, apparently trying to determine if I was telling the truth. Then satisfied, he didn't say a word but waved us on.

We rode on and I explained to George and Hosi what the conversation entailed. George uttered "Holy Shit," while Hosi continued cursing. "Well George," I said, "we swore this was to be our last trip, and I damn sure meant it." George was silent and then responded, "Amen, brother."

We entered Tangiers and George and I immediately completed the transactions, while Hosi secured the jeep. Between us we exchanged approximately $9,200. Again we received over a hundred francs more than the dollar brought in Casablanca. Hosi was shocked at where the money was stashed, hell-over half the trip he was leaning on the gas can.

We piled into the jeep and as I said, "Lets blow this town," Hosi barked, "Aren't we going to look around for a while." George came out of his seat, "Listen Hosi, we've got nine grand on us, and we sure as hell don't want to travel through the mountains after dark, relax and sit back." George was pissed, but he voiced my sentiments exactly.

We made one ill-fated stop for a six-pack and sandwiches on the outskirts of town. There, while waiting for the food, Hosi became friendly with a very attractive lady of the evening. I was unaware of the incident as I was outside, guarding the jeep. It was a military edict, in Morocco, that all vehicles are guarded while off base, punishable by court marshal.

George exited with the food and informed me about Hosi and his new found friend. Soon the "lovely couple" walked toward the jeep with Hosi carrying a suitcase. "Where the hell are you off to with the suitcase, I asked?" Now I was getting pissed. Then he laid a sob story on George and I that her pimp was treating her badly, and she wanted to "relocate" in Casablanca, a much larger city. "You mean more men, especially GIs, I blurted out." She didn't understand English and kept babbling in Spanish to Hosi, while Hosi continued pleading her case. "She didn't have a family and had very few friends, thus she desperately wanted out of Tangiers," he added. I looked at George, he shrugged, it was ok with him. I looked back at her trying to guess her nationality as something was bugging me, but one thing was certain, with her looks and body, she would become very wealthy in Casablanca. Finally I faced Hosi and said, "If she causes any problems, it's her ass that's on the line" He agreed, and so did a very tense George.

The four of us rode on with the "love-birds" chattering away in Spanish accompanied with hugs and kisses. It was a beautiful day as we ascended the Rif Mountains and approached Rasheed's Park, as George named it. Sure enough the "Welcome Party" was waiting, much to my chagrin. "Shit," I said, "We're outta cigarettes." "No we're not," George muttered, "I bought five cartons when we got sandwiches." "Good Old George, he came through again," I thought.

I brought the jeep to a halt and George became busy opening cigarette cartons and passing out packs. Rasheed was smiling as he approached the vehicle, then froze-the smile was gone-and he grabbed my arm. "Who she," he hissed. Quietly I explained that she was a friend of Hosi, the airman in the back seat, and wanted a ride to Casablanca.

Rasheed's top lip curled up in a sneer, "She whore," he spat "and a Jewess." I recoiled at his words, a whore, yes but a Jew? Through my brain thundered the Arab-Jew relationship for the last three thousand years, give or take a week. I cursed Hosi. Rasheed ordered the girl out of the jeep and Hosi followed her. Rasheed walked up to her, his face inches from hers, and spat "You Jew!"

She cringed and started bawling, as it became apparent she understood French. Then she turned and looked at Hosi pleadingly, who attempted to step between her and Rasheed but George immediately grabbed Hosi and hurled him back towards the jeep. Geirge's fast action did not go unnoticed by Rasheed and his men. "This is not our war," he screamed at Hosi. "Frank warned you that if she caused problems, it was her ass." "But," Hosi pleaded. "But my ass" interrupted George, "you dumb shit, look around us. There are thirty armed guerrillas and we haven't even got a peashooter!"

The girl was terrified, and rightfully so. I noticed that the guerrilla band had encircled us, the situation was indeed tense. I asked, somewhat lamely, "what was the problem?" He replied, "She is a Jew and the Amerikans stay out." Once again I asked if I could help, but Rasheed turned and faced me with a very menacing glare, "Leave," he said, "but the whore stays."

I repeated his words that stunned both George and Hosi. George recovered immediately, "Hey, we're outnumbered, they're armed, its not our country or our war, and Frank warned the both of you, I say lets go!" Hosi started some plaintive argument about "Americans and duty" but I cut him short. "Listen you bastard, I've had enough of your bullshit, it was your hot pants that caused the entire incident." Then I got right in his face and asked, "Did you know that she was Jewish?" "Yea," he replied, "so what."

"Hosi," I replied, "Take a few weeks off and read the history of the religious conflicts in this part of the world and wise up. We're leaving now, no heroics or I swear, we'll leave without you." We climbed into the jeep, the girl was screaming and wailing, while Hosi was muttering something under his breath. I did feel sorry for her, but drove off, never looking back. What happened to her remains a mystery. I feel certain she was never raped, as Berbers consider Jews "unclean." She probably ended up a slave.

Several miles down the road, Hosi launched into a cursing diatribe calling George and I every foul name he could think of. George now became irate and reaching under his seat, pulled out a previously undisclosed .25 Beretta automatic and fired one round past Hosi-through the pull down flap area. "The next one, you bastard, is going through your hide," he screamed. Needless to say, Hosi was quiet for the rest of the trip. In fact, he never spoke to me again.

Finally, we reached the friendly confines of Nouasseur AFB. Right after distributing the money to very grateful GIs I went to the First Sergeant's office. After giving him his money, I related the details of both trips. I went into great detail concerning Rasheed and advised that further trips should be aborted, he agreed. Concerning the girl, he said we did the right thing, as considering the odds and weaponry, any other action would have been senseless. As I rose to leave, he asked one more question, "Where the hell did you hide the money?" I replied and he commented, "Nice job."

THE SEAMAN'S CLUB
CASABLANCA, FRENCH MOROCCO, 1955

Casablanca was not a city noted for entertainment during the years 1955-1956. A civil war was raging in the countryside and getting closer to the city every day. The Moroccan people desperately wanted independence from France, and the war had decidedly tilted in their favor. This turn of events was startling as camel-borne Berber tribesmen were routing an army equipped with tanks and jet aircraft. Thousands of French and Jewish inhabitants were seeking refuge in the major coastal cities of Tangiers, Rabat and Casablanca. Once there, many planned to emigrate. Even the French Foreign Legion was being driven back from the hinterland.

Sgt. Jesse Harmon and I were assigned to the Oued Zem tanker off-loading facility in the northern sector of Casablanca. There, along with Lt. Mesnick, we comprised a cadre of three bold and very isolated GI's in the Casablanca enclave. The Nouasseur AFB was 30 kilometers distant. Fortunately, Jesse and I lived in a different hotel than the Lieutenant, and this provided for complete freedom to explore the city at night.

We had already visited countless bars featuring belly dancers and opium dens in the French and Arab districts, but continued to search for other diversions to satisfy our bizarre appetites. While the rioting in the streets and general unrest made daily traveling hazardous, we continued our quest. It was at lunch time one day that we hit the jackpot. Needing a fast lunch, we traveled only nine city blocks when we espied the Seaman's Club.

It was a large establishment located on a wharf. Inside was a very long bar that seated sixty- seventy patrons, plus many tables that were scattered helter-skelter. The place appeared disorganized, and all bottles, liquor and otherwise, were securely hidden behind the bar. It was obvious that the visiting clientele were a special breed. Behind the bar a posting of merchant ship arrivals caught my eye that portended evenings of exciting entertainment. I quickly scanned the information. Two days hence, five ships were due to arrive from Hong Kong, Malaysia, Holland, Poland and England. That meant five crews, who had just spent weeks, perhaps months at sea toiling on ill equipped merchant vessels, developing rapacious thirsts for alcohol, were going to descend upon this bar. Jesse and I smiled and vowed to be present.

We arrived on the appointed day early, as we wanted special seats. Then we each ordered four beers and found the farthest corner, which was elevated, to watch the unfolding spectacle. The beers would get warm, but we had no desire to reenter the bar area once the crews arrived.

Merchantmen worked late upon docking at a new port, so we sat back and waited. The ship's captains wanted as much work as possible completed before they released their parched crews to prowl the bars. Our expectations of the evening's activities were not disappointed. The various crews arrived, stormed the bar, and naturally, everyone demanded to be served first. Dozens of languages and dialects could be heard. Some men had cut-off shirts, some were bare chested; black men, white men, yellow men-a menagerie of the human race thronged the bar. Dress codes and chivalry were not the order of the day!

It didn't take long before the first fight started. Initially it was only a few men, but what brought down the house was when one crew fought another, which frequently occurred. It was a melee to behold; shouting, cursing, fists and bottles flying-a real donnybrook.

Management, which we noted were all robust men, made no attempt to interfere. They let the fight continue until the crewmen got tired. Slowly the broken bodies on the floor mounted, then the battle slowly subsided. Fractured arms and legs were common, as was extensive facial damage, but after a few more rounds of booze, the situation returned to normal. Quite often we saw crewmen aiding their fallen comrades back to their ship. In the many times we viewed these scenes, we never observed a fatality-was it luck or thick skulls, we wondered!

Soon the hour arrived when everyone was too drunk to fight. At that point, Jesse and I would sneak out of the bar and fade into the night until the next time. This generally occurred after two or three hours of non-stop activity. The

Seamen's Club was certainly unique. I have never seen a bar, before or since, whose patrons guaranteed trouble, and it was acceptable.

THE DEVIL'S BRIGADE
THE FRENCH FOREIGN LEGION-1955

Throughout their history, the Legion's feats are synonymous with courage and tenacity against hopeless odds. The Legionnaires were thrust against the Patet Lao in Asia, and confronted Algerian Tribesmen, in the Sahara Desert. They were at Timbuktu and defied the siege of Diem Bien Phu. Now their foes were the Berber tribesmen of the Atlas and Rif Mountains in Northern Africa. Legionnaires were the personification of the word "mercenary," and in the Moroccan Civil War of 1955-56, they were France's last resolve to thwart the Moroccan desire for independence.

I had met several of their cadres during excursions in the Moroccan countryside. They were manning various roadblocks, seeking insurgents, while I was a casual jeep driver visiting petroleum-pumping stations for the three huge American air installations in Morocco. No more than a few words passed between us; they were strangers in a foreign land as was I. Their faces revealed that their pact with the Devil was sealed and future atrocities could not further darken their souls. On leaving them, however, I retained a seared memory sketch of their blank, haunting visages. The dull listless eyes seemingly lacked hope or feeling and imparted a forlorn reminder of being the ultimate outcast. Then they became real people one hot July afternoon in a bar on Rue Bullet in Casablanca.

I was out for a stroll through Casablanca against the sound advice of all my friends. They repeatedly cautioned me concerning my habit of exploring the city alone. After all they implored, there was a civil war raging! I insisted on mingling among the people, how better to understand their plight? Many times on these sojourns I would stay at another hotel for the night, which drove my friends into frenzy.

This particular hot afternoon I entered a bar for a cold beer. I had walked a considerable distance and felt ready for a cool libation. I entered the Café Rouge and decided on a seat in the center of the bar that seated approximately twenty people. At strange bars it was always my rule not to sit at the end seats if possible. Too often it was at the end of the bar that trouble started, thus I was leery. I ordered a Stork beer, it was locally-brewed and nicknamed by GIs "Crackerjack Beer"-a surprise in every bottle. It was the beer of preference, as American or European beers were not always available. I received my beer and before I savored the first sip, the entrance door was flung open with a crash and approximately ten-fifteen legionnaires stormed in. The patrons on both sides of me immediately vacated their seats and scurried to the rear of the establishment, cowering with trepidation. This reaction, I was to learn, was the unspoken rule of the Legionnaires and the local populace didn't argue. I, being fully attired in my military uniform, which was mandatory for All-American military personnel, remained motionless as the seats to my right and left became occupied with Legionnaires. Quietly I sipped my beer, while being closely scrutinized by the new customers.

All the Legionnaires appeared to be German, whose ages were approximately between 40-50. They also all had facial hair, beards and mustaches. These men offered a fierce presence that left no doubt that they were prepared for any encounter. The men were fully armed, sub-machine guns were placed on the bar for easy access, and every belt was strung with hand grenades. They spoke a German dialect and I assumed them to be remnants of Field Marshall Ervin Rommel's elite Afrika Corps that dealt many defeats to the Allied Army during World War II. They obviously remained in Africa after the war for personal reasons. I had also read in the local newspapers that Arabs targeted single Legionnaires for attack, thus the Legionnaires now traveled in squads, fully armed, even to get a beer.

I addressed the man to my right in French. He responded and I took his lead as he spoke softly in a subdued manner, not wishing to be overheard. He was of German extraction and I was the first American he had ever spoken to. I was very careful in my conversation and never questioned his background or birthplace. I remarked that I hadn't seen Legionnaires in Casablanca before. He responded that the war was lost and all outlying forces were being driven to the coast where an embarkation would occur. I was intrigued by the conversation and extended it by buying the Legionnaire a beer. He gratefully accepted and we talked on about the countryside, the mountains and the cruel Sahara Desert. These men were outcasts, many of whom might be war criminals and thus unable to return home for fear of retribution-men essentially without a country.

During our conversation, I closely scrutinized his comrades. They were all embattled German veterans, tired wary men whose only opportunity for survival rested in the comradeship of their fellow Legionnaires. Many exhibited various scars and tattoos; they were truly the most fearsome group of assassins I ever encountered. The men spoke little, laughed less and were constantly peering around for some unseen enemy.

These men were caught in a time warp. Ten years out of World War II, which they lost-now engaged in someone else's Civil War, which was being lost-far from a homeland who had forgotten them-all they knew was killing.

Gradually our conversation halted as the Legionnaire became sullen and silent. Slowly I arose, as any quick movement would be unwelcome. The Legionnaire on my right looked at me and raised his glass in quiet salute. Fleetingly our eyes met, and I departed. As I opened the door I glanced back; every Legionnaire had his eyes on me. There before me I was watching a brief niche of time, a tiny slice of history. Quietly I exited.

BIRTH OF A NATION
THE OASIS IN CASABLANCA, 1956

It was an oasis amid the chaos of a civil war in a country rebelling against the colonial rule of France. From 1953 to 1956, Morocco was ablaze with insurgency, and Casablanca, the largest city, was a caldron of seething unrest. The French Foreign Legion was being forced to withdraw to the coast abandoning the vast interior to the native population. Independence for Morocco was in the wind, and the elixir of freedom was the drink every Moroccan savored. Amidst the unrest stood the L'otel Gentilhommerie, located at 17 Rue Bullet in the southeastern section of Casablanca. There, five Americans, in some inexplicable roll of the dice, found an enclave for philosophical debate, camaraderie and safety.

Jesse H. was my roommate at Nouasseur and became a very interesting individual as time progressed. He was about six feet and stocky, a solid farm boy away from home for the first time. At nineteen years of age, he spoke very little except about his girl back home. We both worked at the petroleum depot's tank farm although our training was vastly different. He was having an affair with Jackie, the secretary at the petroleum tank farm, who was nearly twice his age. Then in June, he and I received notification that we were being transferred to the port facility in Oued Zem, a suburb of Casablanca. I was on a trip to Tangiers at the time, and I nearly flipped when I heard the details. We were each to receive $165.00 a month off base living allowance, an unbelievable amount, plus we had our own jeep for transportation. I was ecstatic and ready to re-enlist. He also informed me that he located two rooms for us in a small, quiet hotel for $35.00 a month. Then he informed me that Jackie also lived there-was I surprised!

The l'otel was a small two-and-a-half story establishment with only seven apartments on the second and third floors and these were occupied. On the first floor, there were three apartments that were usually empty, as was customary in almost all-public and private buildings in Moroccan cities. The buildings permitted free public access to the first floor, and at night, it belonged to the street people, as all movable items were secured. However, as expediency demanded to be near friends, Jesse had rented one of the apartments for me and many nights the turning of my doorknob prompted me to grasp the stiletto under my pillow.

The third story portion had an exit to the rooftop of the second floor which the residents used as a large patio. There, in the comfort of chairs, chaise lounges, iced beverages and potted palms, the resident expatriates were secure from the turmoil of the streets and could safely observe the burning desire of rebellion.

The Moroccan War for Independence was a spectacle to behold. Sparked by the Berber tribesmen, whose refuge lay in the Rif and Atlas Mountains, a constant war of attrition was conducted against a far-better-equipped French adversary. It was rifles and scimitars of the Berber horse and camel cavalry versus jet planes and tanks. The clandestine war was conducted utilizing hit and run tactics; it was a war to undermine French confidence and morale while depleting the coffers of Paris. Raids were carried out at night, and they inflicted terror among French sympathizers after which, the raiders vanished into the mountains.

The Moroccan seaport cities of Tangiers and Casablanca were besieged by the influx of settlers, mainly Jewish and French from the countryside, who sought emigration These settlers were harassed by Moroccan nationals for being pro-French and anti-independence. Thus the streets were crowded with travelers utilizing every imaginable mode of transportation filled with personal belongings. The cacophony of the streets was unbelievable.

We Americans occupied five of the ten apartments at the hotel. The other three, on the second floor, were rented by ever-changing European clientele. Jesse had a second floor apartment while on the third floor resided Jackie, Muriel and a Californian named Choy.

Choy worked at Nouasseur AFB as a cook at the Officer's Club, while Muriel and Jackie were employed as a teacher and secretary at the base. They were both from Oklahoma, daughters of wealthy oil families and graduates of the University of Oklahoma. They both loved poetry and read philosophy constantly, their favorite being Friedrich Nietzsche, the German philosopher. Previously, I had only read a smattering of his works. but after a few months of discussing philosophical issues on the roof, I read his two major works, "The Antichrist and Thus Spake Zarathustra."

Both women had lurid backgrounds; Muriel was a lesbian and Jackie was bi-sexual It was because of these sexual preferences that their families, both devoted Southern Baptist, "requested" that the women relocate. They were in there twenties when the ouster occurred. Now, after wandering for over a decade, Jackie was thirty-eight and Muriel was pushing forty-four.

I was at a total loss concerning sexual appetites and the drug culture but Casablanca introduced me to both. I met my first homosexual, an Air Force Corporal who was Roman Catholic, during my second month at Nousseur while on an R&R trip to Gibraltar. He hesitatingly informed me how frustrated and sad he was concerning his dilemma. Now I encountered the first lesbian and bisexual personages I'd ever known. As far as drugs were concerned the Medina, the old Arab section, was rampant with opium dens to which my curiosity carried me many times, but only to observe the depth of depravity to which man can sink. Thus my education concerning social vices was broadening immensely.

Jackie and Muriel were still bed partners and Jesse's intrusion did not create any difficulties. Muriel realized that

Jackie possessed nymphomania desires and could do little
to interfere. In addition, Jackie and Muriel maintained
their relationship with Jesse's understanding. It was a weird
"menage-a-trois." For the kid from Ronco, Pa. however,
these shenanigans were a real eye-opener.

Jackie and Muriel had come to Morocco in 1954 and
were pondering their next move when Jesse entered the
picture. Now, all three were looking ahead, while I, the
observer, just looked on. Both women liked me, and we
had many intriguing conversations concerning literature
and philosophy. It was the first time I'd ever encountered
anyone who shared my literary and philosophical interests, and I enjoyed our discussions.

Jackie was completely altering Jesse's personality, his
speech, mannerisms and even his thinking process. I observed the change of a Tennessee hillbilly to an individual
who readily discussed world events. The transformation
was remarkable, and it was obvious that Jesse was pleased.
He informed me that at first he didn't like the Yankee who
bunked next to him. He couldn't understand my love of
science and literature.

Jesse was due to be discharged two months after our
tour of duty in Morocco, but he confided in me that he
planned to extend his tour of duty. He wanted to remain
in Casablanca with Jackie, he was mesmerized with her,
and his high school sweetheart had long faded from the
scene. I cautioned him to question the wisdom of his decision, as did Jackie, but he was insistent.

The time I stayed at the L'otel Gentilhommerie was intriguing. It was similar to observing a Greek tragedy as

each unbelievable scene was played out. I was a shadow entity watching the entire drama.

Choy and I eventuality became good friends. He was from California, spoke Chinese and English equally well and maintained the reticence innate to Orientals. Also, he possessed an absolutely inscrutable face; I felt that I never knew what he was thinking, but on occasion I witnessed a twinkle in his eyes that revealed his bewilderment of American antics. Choy owned a Volkswagen Beetle that was often crammed with Chianti and food for the five of us, as we engaged in weekend excursions despite the civil war raging in the countryside. It was the type of bizarre indulgences that we engaged in, as if we were impervious to injury. We were often stopped by military patrols and warned of danger, but drove on protected by our innocence or ignorance. Mazagan was a frequent stop. It was an opulent resort town located on the coast and the playground for the rich. Agadir was our longest trek, approximately three hundred miles distant. The Portuguese founded Agadir in 1500 as a fortress to protect Portuguese fishing interests. In 1960, three and-a-half years after my exit, two earthquakes devastated the town. Estimates of fatalities reached 12,000.

The abject poverty of the countryside overwhelmed me. Electric power was not available, thus refrigeration and associated amenities were nonexistent. To see a meat market was gut-wrenching, as it consisted of a cow or goat hanging in a park from a tree, in 90+ degree heat, covered with flies until someone ordered a piece of meat. Then the "butcher" slapped the side of the carcass with a large carving knife, and as the flies rose, he would cut off the desired portion. I felt sorry for the new King, as the French were obviously losing the war and the Moroccan people expected an immediate transformation to occur after the war was won. The populace expected the change, from chaos to Eden in several days, a week at most. I replied that perhaps a century was needed to transform the nation, but my words were incomprehensible and fell on deaf ears.

Jesse and I found our daily trips to work getting exceedingly more difficult. Frenzied mobs jammed the street every day and made passage difficult. GIs, at Nouasseur AFB, were notified that Casablanca was off-limits, but for us it was a series of daily confrontations.

At the L'otel Gentilhommerie, the street demonstrations and noise meant more parties on "the roof." We would lie back on our lounge chairs, sipping Chianti or bourbon, and observe the demonstrations on the street below. Good or bad, we were watching the creation of a new nation, thus we lifted our glasses in tribute. Hemingway would have been proud, as we expatriates were conscious but silent observers.

Finally, in March of 1956, Independence Day arrived. Sultan Mohammed V became ruler of "The Kingdom of Morocco" which included Spanish Morocco and the Tangiers enclave. His residence was in the ancient city of Rabat, located approximately fifty miles north of Casablanca, on the coast. Rabat is an old city, Moslem in makeup but Moorish in architecture and decidedly less modern or "European."

Casablanca was now a scene of volcanic madness. It was announced that the Sultan was coming by train in a specially built car for the occasion. All work was canceled due to impending crowds; thus I left our hotel early, armed with my 35mm camera to photograph for posterity. The large square, dividing the Washington Hotel and the Medina was jammed with thousands of Moroccans.

Armed mounted soldiers were everywhere. The scene was one of madness and confusion plus, the noise was deafening but I didn't mind, it was history.

It was a mosaic of life. Turbans and djellabas were everywhere, veiled women in robes, desert tribesmen on horseback, all to meet their Monarch. The train arrived, the Sultan stepped out on a prepared platform, and the crowd went berserk-especially the women who issued that eerie Arab cry emanating from the clicking of the tongue.

After an hour, a large area in the square was cleared near the train to be used as a salutation site for the desert horsemen, Berbers and others. They would charge the train, on camel or horse, rear up in their saddles and yell some Moroccan war chant, then charge away. Wave after wave performed this ritual. These men brandishing rifles, scimitars and other antiquated weapons fascinated me for they had defeated a world power, France. It was a classic example of desire overcoming adversity, antiquated weapons over jets and tanks; truly a scene from the Arabian Knights.

Several of the desert warriors, on camels, stopped near me. They were clothed from head to foot in robes except for their eyes, and then I noticed them. I had read about this particular tribe whose top portion of the cornea was darkened from the constant radiation of he sun. Indeed, they were menacing.

With many mixed emotions, I left the square and eventually arrived back at the Oasis, as the streets were becoming impassable. Slowly, deep in thought, I climbed the stairs, attempting to digest what I just observed, but I realized it would require time to fully comprehend; thus I joined the Independence Day Party that was in high gear. We all lifted a glass to independence and remained on the roof throughout the night. That night, as usually was the occasion, we listened to Frank Sinatra's "Wee Small Hours of the Morning" while watching history unfold before us. We actually wore out one album and were working on the second.

Several days later I received bad news, I was being transferred to 17th Air Force Headquarters in Rabat. I was devastated, I enjoyed life in Casablanca. The new Petroleum Office was to be staffed, initially, with only four individuals, A Col. Cox, M/Sgt. Chet H., and two "gofers," me and old friend George M. I had to go, I realized that, but at least "ole pal" George was going along. George immediately dubbed the four of us, "Cox's Army."

My last week in Casablanca was one never-ending party. Many days, the Muezzin calling the faithful to prayer awakened me, as I slept in a wicker chair outside on the roof. Jesse still insisted that he would return to Casablanca after being discharged, but I doubted him, as time and distance are bedfellows to reason.

Three months later I again received another bolt out of the blue; I was being transferred to Tripoli, Libya. Apparently my request for transfer, made during my first week at Nouasseur in the presence of an "incredulous First Sgt." who roared "never, you're here for two years like everyone else," was still in effect. I phoned Jesse and asked for one more rooftop party before I left Morocco, and he readily agreed. Talking to Jesse, I marveled at the change Jackie had wrought, he was indeed "another man."

I decided to travel by train to Casablanca, and I embarked on the strangest train ride of my life. George warned me and said I was "nuts." The train was packed with people, goats, sheep and luggage of every conceivable type. The roofs of the train cars were packed with people also, but at least they had fresh air. The stench inside my car was sickening; it indeed was a foul smelling trip.

I was the only American aboard the train. There were a few Frenchmen but the rest were Moroccan. We finally reached Casablanca and "the gang" was all there to greet me and once in Choy's Beetle, Jackie passed me an open bottle of champagne-it tasted delicious. What a weekend, "what a party," as the entire two days were spent on the roof. All of the World's problems were solved that weekend. Books, philosophy and life were discussed amid the clinking of glasses. Chianti, bourbon and vodka flowed.

When I departed on Sunday, we realized we would never meet again; we had become good friends despite immense differences in character and philosophy. Perhaps the turmoil that surrounded us forged the camaraderie, but I would never forget "The Oasis." The ride back to Rabat was deja-vu; it smelled just as bad.

In 1959, three years after leaving Casablanca, on a whim I wrote a letter to Jackie Walker c/o L'otel Gentilehommerie, 17 Rue Bullet. I was now attending Penn State and realized that a response was improbable; but I was shocked as I did receive one. It was from Jackie and was a short note informing me that Jesse had indeed extended his tour of duty but had to return to the states to get discharged at Ft. Dix. He then caught the next flight to Casablanca, and they were living together at her old apartment; Jesse never returned to Tennessee or corresponded with his family. Muriel and Choy had moved on; she was now working at an Air Force Base in Ankara, Turkey, and Choy was at a base in Germany. Jackie and Jesse had no firm plans, but needed to move somewhere as the Air Force had announced the closure of all Moroccan bases.

I often think of that brief six-month education at 17 Rue Bullet. If I could learn as much in every six month period, I would.......

ONE GLIMPSE OF LONG AGO
SABRATHA, LIBYA-JUNE 20, 1956

The amphitheater has long been silent. The final curtain is but a shroud of dust on a barren stage. No more do eloquent orations emanate, and the last bows have long been offered. The final lines are obscured by the whispers of the Siroccan Wind and lie buried in the desert sands. Around me the ghosts of an ancient audience sit motionless and silent awaiting the next act.

I sit, a solitary visitor, high on a stone seat of the magnificent amphitheater in Sabratha, Libya one hot June afternoon in 1956. Under a cerulean sky, I study the artistry carved in the golden structure of rock and limestone exhibiting beautiful Justinian mosaics and aquatic figurines. The golden arches of center stage frame a portal through which the sapphire Mediterranean Sea can be seen in a distance. The ravages of time have now reduced the stage to a single tier as the upper three are buried in the rubble.

Sabratha lies 40 miles west of Tripoli in the arid, desolate province of Tripolitania. Founded by Carthaginians in 400 BC, it was conquered and rebuilt by the Roman Empire in 150 BC. Sabratha was one of three Roman bastions built in Libya during this period. Oea (Tripoli) and Leptis Magna were the other two cities that formed the emporia. The three enclaves were built on the Mediterranean coast, clinging to the narrow strip of greenery that separates the Sea from the utter desolation of the Sahara Desert.

I had arrived at Sabratha on a crowded, old doddering bus along with 30 other tourists from Wheelus Air Force Base in Tripoli. The temperature was a sweltering 110 degrees and a portent of a further discomforting day was prophesied when, as we approached Sabratha, the bus driver ordered, "All windows must be shut immediately!" The purpose of this insanity, on a bus without air conditioning, became clear as the bus chugged to a halt and was immediately besieged by swarms of flies.

The climate of this area of Tripolitania is very hot; so hot the common honeybee can not subsist, as the heat prevents the honeycombs from becoming firm. Thus no honey means no bees, which means no pollination; ergo pollination occurs only by accident-via flies! The poor sanitation facilities and the open-air markets that abounded throughout the region greatly enhanced the quantity of flies. Also, to add to the misery, the local government had banned the killing of flies in an attempt to increase the probability of accidental cross-pollination. During my day's visit, I must confess, I never saw one fly swatted. The reputation of Arabic Law (or lack thereof) was well understood.

The ruins of Sabratha are truly awe-inspiring. A testament to time and Man's creativity. I spent the entire afternoon walking and examining, my camera dutifully recording the sights. Statues of headless torsos stood guard throughout, disfigured by vandals over the centuries. Most of these sculptural specimens stood seven to ten feet high. However it was the golden amphitheater that was the centerpiece, and it captured my attention time and again. Nearby were many smaller structures, including baths and sculpted columns, which once supported some long disintegrated building. The dry hot climate had preserved the remains very well.

At the end of our tour I dashed aboard the sweltering bus and almost welcomed the heat, as the flies were left outside. Temporarily seated alone, I attempted to digest the spectacle I had just beheld and reflected upon the history that transpired here. I realized that the probability of my viewing ruins of this magnitude and beauty again were very doubtful, thus I took one long, last, searching look through the window at the ruins, in a futile attempt to permanently embed the scene in my brain. However I was inarguably certain that the enormity of the spectacle precluded this possibility. Then the bus departed, and after a few miles, every window flew open.

Returning to Tripoli, I received one more glimpse of the past, as the bus passed Tripoli's most famous landmark-it should be,it's been there since 170 AD-the Roman Arch of Marcus Aurelius.

RUNNING OF THE BULLS
PAMPLONA, SPAIN-1956

Local and tourist thrill-seekers have been running the bulls (Encierro) at Pamplona to celebrate the fiesta of San Fermin for nearly 400 years. It is an event in which the entire population of Pamplona rabidly participates. The festivities commence on July 7 and continue till July, 14th during which time the population of Pamplona swells by thousands, as the influx of tourists is constant. The pageantry and tumultuous celebrations of the event are legend, centered on the daily running of the bulls and culminating with daily corridas.

I was stationed at Wheelus AFB, in Tripoli, Libya in July 1956 when I learned that an R&R trip was scheduled for Madrid, Spain commencing on July 5th. When I read the posting, my legs became weak with anticipation. Would I possibly have the opportunity to witness the event in Pamplona? I was familiar with the spectacle as I had previously devoured Ernest Hemmingway's books on the topic, "The Sun Also Rises" and "Death in the Afternoon". I immediately dashed to the orderly room to sign-up, praying that the flight wasn't already filled. The Gods smiled upon me that day, as I made the roster for the trip.

During the flight I was shocked to learn that I couldn't find one guy who was going to Pamplona; everyone was content to stay in Madrid. I had to agree that Madrid offered plenty of entertainment and history, but to be this close and at this time to Pamplona was to me, a miracle. I finally convinced two adventuresome characters to join me in my excursion. If I hadn't, I would have gone anyway, but I preferred to have a couple of GIs with me. We landed and immediately John D, Henry S. and I boarded a bus for Pamplona, which is approximately 210 miles northeast of Madrid.

We arrived at approximately 7 p.m. on July 6th. Checking our meager luggage in a locker at the bus station, where it remained for three days, we quickly got swept up with the festivities. The air was electric with anticipation as the large crowds surged through the streets, and soon we were enveloped in the spontaneity of the moment. Our uniforms were a blessing as we received many free drinks; beer and especially-wine. Soon we purchased our own goatskin wine bags and mastered the art of drinking from them. Around 2 a.m., three-quarter's drunk, we decided to sleep-anywhere. Henry's suggestion sounded appropriate, and certainly the most financially sound, thus we ended up on three park benches.

At sunup the next morning, three bleary-eyed GIs were awakened by the roar of the crowd, as many were continuing to party, while others were starting anew. The crowds were already jamming the streets, heading towards the starting gate were the bulls would be released. Rising unsteadily we gingerly followed the crowd nursing hangovers, very severe hangovers, as only those created from wine can be. It was nearly 7 a.m. and the wine was flowing, soon our maladies were a thing of the past, set on the shelf for a day as we indulged in the grape.

The spectacle of the Running of the Bulls and Corridas, is steeped in legend, however a great deal of authenticity supports the legend. At Knossos, in Crete, a wall painting dates from approximately 2000 BC depicts men confronting bulls. The conquering Moors, in approximately 711 AD, had ritualistic occasion on feast days to confront bulls, while on horseback, and kill them. In August of 1385, by Royal Order of Carlos II, a modern form of bullfighting was inaugurated in Spain. The Corridas of today are the same since 1726, when Francisco Romero of Ronda, Spain introduced the estoque (sword), and the muleta (the small worsted cape), used in the finale of the fight.

Finally the hour of insanity arrived, 8 a.m. to run or not to run? To me the prerequisites were obvious. One-the runners had to be young, thus in good physical condition. Two-the runners had to be foolish or crazy. Three-the important ingredient, the runners must be intoxicated. Thus, we three GI's agreed that we were eminently qualified, but the question remained, did we have the testicular fortitude to do it. Several more gulps of wine settled the issue; it was go!

It has been written that between July 7-July 14th the entire male population of Pamplona is comprised of psychopaths and/or masochists. We three Americans did nothing to change these assumptions.

Slowly we climbed down the barricade-after filling our goatskin wine bags. We positioned ourselves about 100 yards from the starting gate-a runner can't be too bold on his first dash to insanity. The street was lined with wooden barricades along its entire 800-metre length from the Town Hall Plaza to the Plaza de Toros. The entire event that was about to transpire would last less than five minutes. Henry and I hung together, while John wandered aimlessly. Up went the wine bags again and again to bolster our courage, but by now we were so tense with anticipation, the wine left us unfazed. I kept thinking of a conversation I heard the previous evening among British tourists, they were commenting that since the 1920s, "only" 10 runners have been killed during the event-very comforting. Then at 8 a.m., a rocket announced that six bulls, all approximately 1500 lb. each, were loose in the streets. A frenzied cheer accompanied this announcement as the crowd roared its approval.

John and I looked at each other, but no reply was needed, we started running. Even though the bulls were approximately 100 yards distant, we didn't plan on waiting. Suddenly I was intoxicated with reality and never was there a grape with a better bouquet. I was actually in Pamplona, the sun had just risen, and behind me were some very angry bulls.

We ran for several eternity's, gasping for breath, but speed on the crowded street was impossible, and I continually heard the noise growing louder, apparently only the bulls had the right-o-way. We kept running and looking for John, but he was not in sight and then I heard it, hooves. Hooves of large, menacing animals that were rapidly getting closer. I looked over at Henry, "I'm bailing out I shouted," to which he replied, "me too." Thus we scaled the barricade with many friendly arms to assist us, generally accompanied with jeers.

Later we learned, as it happens every year, several runners got gored. Finally, in the climax of a very memorable day, we watched several bullfights at the plaza de toros, which I found exhilarating. It is Spain's ritual and I applaud their choice. We finally located John and he informed us that he ran the entire distance, I guess he was drunker than Henry and I.

Since participating in the running and witnessing the subsequent events, I look upon the spectacle of bull fighting with reverence and admiration. But one of the matador's movements will always remain embedded in memory. It is the classical cape maneuver by the matador, called the "Veronica." It was named for the woman who supposedly held out a cloth and wiped Christ's face on his way to his crucifixion.

The trip was everything I fathomed it to be, even in the remote recesses of my mind. It was a visit to history, pageantry, nihilism, and a drink with Bacchus.

HE WAS AN HONEST CROOK
CAPE CANAVERAL, FL. 1957

It was a seizure of incredulity. The photograph leaped at me, defying me to identify the individual. At first, stunned, I stared in disbelief at the caption over the photo," WANTED for MURDER and BANK ROBBERY." There in the photo was my old friend and pinochle partner at Cape Canaveral, Cy Rosetti of New York. Apparently, Cy did what we at the Cape thought he was kidding about; he fulfilled his intention and lived a life of crime.

I was in the small post office of Unionville, Centre County, Pa. Actually, the post office was one half of someone's house as is the case in Smalltown, USA. I was present because of a strange series of events.

The time was July of 1959 and I was attending Penn State University for a summer class of Logic that I needed for graduation. As always, I was short of cash, so I did some creative renting at the nearby Black Moshannon State Park where my lodging consisted of a tent, swimming area, bathrooms and lantern light, all for $3.00 a week. One night while listening to Radio Hamilton, Ontario the host read a poem that caught my attention and I wanted a copy. That night I wrote a letter to the station requesting it and the next day I went to the nearest post office to mail it and arrange picking up my correspondence. It was there that I learned of my friend's activities.

Cy and I arrived in Florida at the same time from two diametrically opposite ends of the spectrum, in geography, philosophy and goals. I had returned from Africa and Cy from Korea. We were billeted in the same barracks, a three-story structure consisting of twenty rooms per floor with two men assigned to a room. We did not room together, but he had the room directly across the hall.

As usual, near the end of the month, all GIs are broke and card games provide a distraction.

During one of the games, usually pinochle, the subject of guns came up and Cy's roommate commented on the guns that Cy brought back from Korea. When asked, Cy showed the three foreign handguns he brought back. When asked what he had in mind for the weaponry, he laughed and replied, "Rob banks, naturally."

My job at Cape Canaveral was that of a Fuel Analyst for the countless missiles that were being launched in the burgeoning US Space Program. I had received my Certificate in Organic Chemistry at the School for Fuel Analysis, a military program, shortly after I entered the Air Force. It was conducted at the gigantic petroleum fuel depot in Newark, NJ by a consortium of Oil Companies in conjunction with the Air Force. Now I was fulfilling a boyhood dream at Cape Canaveral. I was in the Space Program.

Cy and I became close friends, not only because of the card games, but he surprised me with his interest in chemicals, especially explosives. He constantly asked about dynamite, nitroglycerin and black powder, their formulation and the difficulty in their manufacture. Finally I took him to a bookstore in Cocoa Beach and selected a book for him to read on the subject. Cy was constantly amazed at the fact that I made black powder and other explosives at age 10 in Ronco, Pa. from my old chemistry set. I became suspect at his intentions, but everything I told him was public knowledge and available in any bookstore.

Cy visited the laboratory where I worked many times during our six-month relationship. The vials, flasks, and mysterious liquids fascinated him. He was like a kid in a candy store. Finally in July 1957, I was discharged and off I went to Penn State. I totally forgot about Cy until that fateful day in that small post office in Unionville when the past returned.

I stayed awake all night staring at the stars, and thinking about Cy and our relationship. I had no regrets of my actions concerning the explosive crash course I'd given him. If not me, someone else would have; there were no secrets that I conveyed to him. In several days I started to forget Cy, as my mind was back on my college studies; in a week I forgot about Cy for twenty-one years.

In 1980, I was the Engineering Manager for the Amperex Industry Microwave Manufacturing Facility in Smithfield, RI. The facility had entered a critical rapid ramp-up phase in high volume manufacturing of magnetrons, the critical core component of microwave ovens. Long hours were demanded of senior personnel to achieve corporate objectives. The plant was a beehive of activity.

I was now separated from my wife of eighteen years and living alone in a motel near the plant; a divorce I felt, was imminent. Thus the evenings were lonely, and I discovered a quiet cocktail lounge in nearby Cumberland, RI, the Cher-le-Monde. The place appealed to me as the clientele were predominately businessmen of my age and very active in various local activities. Soon I was frequenting the establishment several evenings a week, making friends while learning about the local business climate.

One of the regulars was a former Chief-of-Police of a nearby town, Joe B. Joe and I became friends, and eventually I rented the lower level of his home, which he recently renovated into an apartment. One evening at the bar, Joe and I were reminiscing about previous strange encounters when I dropped the bombshell.

I mentioned the Wanted Poster I saw twenty-one years earlier at Unionville, PA. The beer was very tasty that evening, and I related the entire story of my relationship with Cy Rosseti. Later I recalled that Joe's face took on an incredulous look, but at the time I felt that it was a policeman's interest. I completed the story and sat back and waited for Joe's comments; however at first, they were not immediately forthcoming.

Joe and I sat there a long time in silence. The only activity was the smoke from our cigars wafting upward, and several of the regulars leaving the establishment, as the usually full bar was rapidly emptying. I got a strange feeling that Joe learned or knew of the case, but he remained silent and he appeared troubled. Then slowly he began speaking, hesitating at first, but then he warmed to the task and revealed to me the final chapters of the life of Cy Rosetti.

It seems that after being discharged from the Air Force, Cy returned to New York City, and with his brother Louie, began a life of crime. Minor at first, but soon the Rosetti brothers were recognized by the NYPD as troublemakers and probably guilty of several robberies, but evidence of their involvement was lacking. The brothers then apparently escalated their activities, and soon were suspected of major felonies.

Then two years after the placid pinochle card games in Florida, an explosion ripped apart a bank vault in the city, and during the daring bank robber's escape a gun battle ensued. Two policemen were shot, and one later died. The bullets were from a foreign-made handgun, very rare in the US and believed to be of Korean origin. The explosives were thought to be of a homemade variety and much too powerful for the job. Evidence suggested that an amateur formulated the explosive mixture.

Apparently the robbers, four in all, split up after they fled, and two were later captured in the dragnet. They identified the other two as the Rosetti brothers. Now a full-fledged manhunt throughout Manhattan and surrounding suburbs was launched.

For several days, photographs of the brothers were splashed across every television newscast and daily newspaper in New York, but no reports of sightings were received by the NYPD. They temporarily vanished, Joe related, because the brothers were hiding out in a deserted warehouse on the lower Eastside. They apparently had food for a few days, but after it was gone, they would canvass the nearest homes in the early morning hours when milk was delivered and steal it. This worked for several days until a cranky Old Italian woman got fed up with the thievery and stayed awake one morning and spotted Cy stealing her bottle of milk. Just as she was about to challenge him she recognized him as the cop killer, stayed indoors and notified the police.

The area was soon swarming with police, and the brothers were on the run. Joe didn't know all the details about their flight, but it led north through Connecticut towards the Rhode Island line. Joe was a RI State Trooper at that time and, being on duty, became involved in the chase. Eventually the brothers were cornered in a farmer's pasture and, refusing surrender decided to shoot it out with the police. Joe admitted, that for the first time as a trooper, he was tense and very concerned as bullets were flying. He had no doubt, he revealed to me, that these guys were desperate killers. The shoot-out ended with Cy shot dead and his brother wounded. Two troopers were "nicked," but otherwise the police were unscathed.

Thus I finally learned about the closure of the Cy Rosetti saga, my card playing partner at Cape Canaveral. It had taken 21years since I saw the Wanted Poster, but now I knew how the curtain finally came down.

I sat there, staring in disbelief at Joe, accepting the tragic finality. When he finished, we were both very silent and sipped our drinks. A half-hour later we left, not a word was spoken as we walked out into the darkened evening.

TO LISTEN-
A DIFFICULT TASK
WILTON, NH

Listen! A difficult task for everyone and only a few understand the issue. We possess all types of excuses, "not now, later, I'm too busy"-we have all used them, unfortunately.

It can be all that a person asks of another, just a moment in time for someone to listen, to ponder their thoughts, ideas or questions. They may be at death's door, on a flight of fantasy, or pleading for mercy. The only request is someone's ear.

To listen, a forgotten fragment of compassion in this helter-skelter world. A child asks to be heard, an inmate questions society's right to judge, or a simple traveler asking directions-they all have a need. All ask for but a moment to have their voice registered on the human scale of assertion. But does anyone listen thoroughly, rarely. Many assume to, but in reality do so only on singular occasions.

What has happened to us human beings that purports our activities so important that someone else's time and dignity are not valuable or worthy of a few seconds. Often times our "listening" doesn't even dignify the query with a pause in our activity, and in haste we do not actually answer the question because we haven't heard it in its entirety. We launch in before the questioner has finished speaking and pour out information that is incorrect, although we possess the right answer if only we had "listened." Why?

One should prepare for the momentous occasion of listening. Cease all activity, face the speaker and devote full attention to the spoken words. Once the idea is practiced it may become infectious. We will have opened a crack in the door. Think of it, we may actually learn something plus impressing the speaker with the fact that he has encountered a unique individual who actually desires to hear his statement.

It is not a rare occasion that we hear a statement and wonder afterwards, "did I hear that correctly, or did they mean something else?" No wonder people hate speeches, they can't justify what they think they heard. Thankfully, the printed word justifies our interpretation or, sadly, is a source of embarrassment. There we can finally determine what was spoken and interpret the statement.

There is a considerable segment of American society that is extremely vulnerable to chicanery and is being fleeced by con men, soothsayers, and questionable religious hoaxes-all fast talkers. These perpetrators of deceit punctuate their orations with "glib quips" that are grasped as gospel by the audience, who ignores the volume of mumbo-jumbo that surrounds it. Once hooked, these individuals are reeled in like fish because of their inability, usually it's their lack of being attentive, to listen. They were so caught up in the speaker's spiel that they weren't listening, just reacting to what they thought the speaker said. This is exactly what the speaker intended. Freedom of speech allows these charlatans to speak, but closed ears and minds permit the damage to occur.

In today's society, subject to mass media verbiage, it is difficult to stay abreast of breaking news stories. Society is inundated with information. Personal research is now mandatory to secure the facts; plus the American media has created a nefarious new ploy at deception-the sound bite. This fragmented encapsulation of a statement or question is a deliberate attempt to confuse the listener or, even more egregious, promote the agenda of another party. These techniques are widely utilized to advance the goals of certain factions of American society and industry, while utilizing the media's resources which they control.

With the media attempting to sway the uninformed and the "too busy to be bothered crowd" which, sad to say, comprise the majority of voters-elections hang in the balance. It is now more critical than ever before to "listen." The species that produced the Murrows, Sevareids and Cronkites are extinct. That era of honest journalism is gone.

Also, another misuse of language has crept into our everyday vocabulary and people have become victimized by their language usage. All encompassing words like "never" and "always" are being bantered about without fully comprehending the finality or magnitude of these words. Any question, statement or conversation that utilizes these words should immediately be suspect; a red flag has been raised. Language is intended for communication but ask yourself this question before you plunge into your next dialogue, "Am I communicating or a part of a deception?"

Listen! Did the august body really understand what Socrates said? Were the American people listening when Eisenhower said, "Beware of the industrial-military complex." Obviously not! But Churchill was emphatically understood when he uttered, "This is their finest hour." Why? Lives were at stake and humanity, as we know it, rested on the outcome. Does it take an Armageddon to occur before we listen?

Tomorrow, try it. When someone speaks, pause, shut your mouth, stop all activity and give attention-listen. It can become contagious.

ECHOES TO REMEMBER
GRIZZLEY LAKE, COLORADO-1966

During my lifetime I have had the good fortune to locate pristine, idyllic sites worthy of revisiting and savoring their beauty. In locating these Edens, I have noticed that often their beauty has been greatly enhanced by Mother Nature, who in agreement with my selections has punctuated the choices by adding an audible statement.

In Canada during my many visits to Lake Opeongo, located in the Algonquin Provincial Park, I was always enraptured by the call of the loon. They offered various intonations, primarily at dusk, when I had laid back to make peace with the world. There, in tranquil meditation, I acknowledged the rhapsody of the wild.

Years later, in Hew Hampshire's mountains, I finally heard the terrifying scream of the eagle, pretentious statement in the wild signifying preeminence over its domain. A chilling cry of defiance, served to all denizens that underscored the presence of the majestic raptor of the sky. To this very day I become tense by the remembrance of that piercing cry.

But my most memorable encounter with this combination of events occurred at 10,200 feet in the Sangre de Cristo Mountains of Colorado. High in the Collegiate Peaks, west of Buena Vista, the site was nestled in Chalk Creek Canyon, three miles straight up from the small village of St Elmo, population 40! Almost all of the visitors to Grizzly Lake, albeit they numbered very few, hiked the three miles but my first visitations occurred with Tom Law, a fellow HP engineer who as a jeep driver in rough terrain was unparalleled. Tom and his jeep made some impossible forays into the wilderness and Ole Griz, as my son and I nicknamed the lake, was one. It was three miles up a very steep grade while transiting three mountain rockslides to the lake, and every inch performed with the jeep's transmission in "granny-low".

Grizzly is situated in a pristine alpine setting surrounded on three sides by soaring snow-capped mountains towering two-three thousand feet overhead. The area teemed with wildlife including Rocky Mountain sheep and cougars. One cougar killed near Buena Vista weighed 160 lb., a big kitty. It was while hiking around "Ole Griz" that I encountered the only wolverine I'd ever seen. Another animal that abounded in the area was elk, which were extensively hunted in the winter when deep snows drove them to lower pastures in search for food.

The most memorable animal, however, was the elusive coyote. Its yelps and howls, often plaintive, serenaded us to sleep most nights. They started howling individually, then answered by others nearby, and soon the canyon rang with a chorus. Lying in the sleeping bag, under the stars, listening to their forlorn calls presented moments for future reminiscences. Even now, some thirty years later, at times when I go to sleep, I recall those blissful moments of quiet meditation, punctuated by the mournful howl of the coyote.

Sleeping bags are a perquisite for trips to Ole Griz. Snow is always a possibility, and we encountered it quite often, even during the Fourth of July weekends. But the night skies are the showcase of wonderment, especially when viewed at a high altitude, as the quantity and clarity of the stars in the Milky Way present a panorama of beauty. It is only then that starlight is truly encountered, as the Milky Way, in all its brilliance, lies before you with the universe as its silent background.

On one trip, my brother George was present, accompanied with two of our nephews, Bob and Ken Helmick. The fishing had been particularly good, and later we dined on the red meat of native cutthroat trout. That particular evening, prior to nodding off, we stared at the incredible expanse overhead. Then we noticed a large bright object passing overhead. George immediately identified it as the Echo Balloon, launched by NASA for experimental purposes. There it hung over the vast Rocky Mountains, seemingly a Christmas ornament, suspended at the fringes of space.

Soon thereafter we heard the call of the coyote, seemingly the fell arch spirit of the wild.

THERE ARE BUT FEW
Taos, New Mexico-1970

There are some individuals who can be identified as "different," outcasts who walk to the beat of a different drummer. They are usually hard to understand, and possess an air about them, not smug or arrogant, just a confident aura of seeing more than is obvious to others. They are artists, poets, sculptors-they are individuals who contribute to the beauty of our world. Scientists also display the same demeanor in their search for truth, but they seek "how" while the artisan questions "why." The similarity has always fascinated by me.

The place was Taos, New Mexico in June 1970. Taos was a small art colony ready to burst onto the American scene as a major center of American art culture. There I was able to observe a special segment of this particular breed of individuals, the artist painter. They appear to combine, in their inner being, the special insights of a shaman with those of a metaphysical physician, and by utilizing these special talents, transfer a vision onto a canvas. It is a scene that many had viewed, but until seen on canvas, through the artist's eyes, never truly appreciated. It is sad that time bestows to so few this remarkable gift.

What is it in a painting that captures a person's eye? Why does a person select "that" painting? There are many similar paintings that abound yet, that "one" is chosen. This situation does not refer to a famous artist's works that are sold for investment, but to the struggling beginner who has not been tainted by money.

I had spent several months searching southern Colorado and northern New Mexico for just "the right painting" to place over my fireplace and was getting frustrated. I had seen many splendid paintings, but there was always something amiss, just not right. Then that fateful day in Taos I espied a particular painting that froze my attention. I looked at it carefully for tens-of-minutes and walked away several times only to return. I had found my painting!

I had selected the painting without ever seeing the artist's name. It was my interpretation of what the artist was conveying, and not his reputation that sold the painting. The scene I saw had extension, history, questions and a story that transcended the canvas.

Today, thirty-one years later and across the continent in New Hampshire, the painting still adorns the place of prominence on our living room wall. Many a day, and especially at night, I stare at the old horse drawn hearse and weather beaten chapel, the saga of the old west, and admire those settlers that endured the test.

The chapel, representing the faith, perseverance and family- the backbone of these settlers, accompanied with grit, guile and determination that were the very essence of the frontier. While the hearse represents adversity, disease, death and finality.

But these are my thoughts, what did the artist see and attempt to convey?

It is apparent from the ethereal colors and shadings that he saw far more then I. Perhaps history was in his thoughts, or was it the future? Was it the downfall of the old West or a portent of times to come? To him, was the vision a beginning or an ending? Perhaps I'll never know, or is that the essence, to contemplate the unknown, the mystery. Is that why we love art, the tantalizing aura of questions and imponderables? Is it the puzzle that attracts us or the pure beauty that captivates our attention?

I shall have this personal inquisition long into the future. At dusk especially, as the last light of day creeps across the painting, I will turn and once again gaze, placing undivided attention upon the scene. Quite often, I delight in knowing that the answer will never be revealed.

IT'S WAR
FALCON ESTATES, COL. -APRIL 1971

In April 1971 I declared war. I had failed miserably the previous four years and if I was to be successful, I had to fight fire with fire. There would be no retreat once I launched my offensive, as I would be unable to stop it. I would fight Mother Nature with her own weapons, and I would employ the most vicious insect in her entomological arsenal. My vegetable garden, after being devoured for four years by aphids, grasshoppers and caterpillars, would be allowed to produce. It was time to bring in the heavy artillery.

My garden was located on a one acre plot of land in Falcon Estates, ten miles north of Colorado Springs, about one half mile east of the south gate to the United States Air Force Academy. The soil wasn't bad for a garden-it was atrocious. It was sand and clay into which I poured four years of manure, and finally it was showing promise. During the previous two years, the plants thrived, only to be devoured by voracious insects.

I was fully cognizant of the dangers that pesticides posed to the welfare of humans and wildlife. DDT had opened everyone's eyes, and Rachel Carson's book "Silent Spring", a favorite reading of mine, had galvanized the public's attention. Thus I turned to a Burpee Seed Catalog for assistance in solving my dilemma. In it I located the two weapons that I planned to utilize, ladybugs and the praying mantis. During my previous five years in Colorado I had not seen one mantis, as it was not indigenous to the area, but I thought if food was plentiful, they might stick around long enough to solve my problem.

Praying Mantis eggs come in cocoons of up to 300, and not having a clue as to what I needed I decided on 3000, and also figured 5000 ladybugs was a nice round number. Thus, with my homework completed, I was prepared to launch my plan.

Coincidentally, Hewlett Packard, my employer, had just launched a new public relations purchasing option program for its employees. After 3 PM, Monday through Friday, an employee could utilize the auspices of HP's purchasing department for personal mail-order items. Thus, armed with my information, I proceeded to visit my friend Lyle Bolender, the buyer.

I had known Lyle for my full five years at HP. We golfed together, played bridge together in the Hewlett Packard Bridge Club with our wives, and on several occasions visited HP vendors to ascertain their capabilities to become suppliers, Lyle representing HP's purchasing department and I represented engineering. Lyle was a loquacious, friendly individual who grasped the importance of situations quickly. His demeanor was molded by his prior military experiences.

Lyle was 50 years old, a retired Army lieutenant colonel who entered the Korean War with the 24th Infantry Division. The 24th Division, consisting of 25,000 men left Pusan, in South Korea and subsequently drove to the Yalu River in North Korea where they engaged the Chinese hordes from the north. Two years later, three truckloads of the 24th Division returned to Pusan representing the entire remnants of the 24th Division. Lt. Col. Lyle Bolender was one of the survivors; he had lived through hell and now the sight of every dawn he considered a bonus.

I sat at Lyle's desk and in a matter-of-fact way, explained to him my dilemma and my solution. I outlined my order for 3000 praying mantis and 5000 ladybug eggs. Lyle was sitting back and listening to my request in disbelief, but with a poker face. After I concluded he remained motionless for about a minute, then broke into peals of laughter that aroused the entire purchasing department. With tears running down his cheek, he shouted, "Frank, I've seen you involved in many crazy engineering experiments, display questionable golf and bridge tactics, but this puts the icing on the cake, you've gone over the edge-you've cracked up." He immediately called his supervisor to witness my request; a man I knew very well, and he too broke into hysterical laughter. The supervisor howled that this purchase order was a first and ordered Lyle to feature the purchase in the company newspaper as "The B̶u̶g̶ Buy of the Month"

Lyle immediately spread the news, concerning my purchase order, throughout the plant. He also made a calendar for his desk, which featured the countdown to "Bugday," the expected delivery date. Soon, people were stopping me and inquiring, many facetiously, but quite a few were honestly interested. Even the Division Manager entered the banter by putting a sign on my desk, parodying Harry Truman, "The Bug Stops Here".

Finally my order arrived, accompanied by horns and hoopla as Lyle "and friends" delivered it to my desk. Lyle even had the Division QA Manager in tow. He presented me with a QA chart that requested a count of bugs that hatched and from which cocoons! It was needed for QA research, he added with a straight face, to determine vendor qualifications.

I placed the eggs in my garden, not too soon, as I noted other insects had arrived. In several days I spotted the first mantis, soon the garden was swarming with "my insects." Watching them devour the insects I was aware that they would be canvassing the neighborhood for additional food. This was fine with me, I was aiding my neighbors I thought; until one day while tending my garden I heard Mrs. Hayden, an elderly divorcee who resided on the adjoining property, scream. "Damn", she shouted to me, "where did all these awful bugs come from? I've lived here five years and never saw them before-they have taken over my patio." Many neighboring women, I learned later, also were terrified and limited their outdoor activities for several weeks. "They're beneficial, I yelled back-they kill the garden and plant pests! That's why I bought them and released them." "You what", she screamed, "only a damn fool would buy three inch long bugs." I immediately realized I'd said too much!

With that closing statement, Mrs. Hayden never spoke to me again during my next eight years as her neighbor; come to think of it, a few other neighbors gave me the cold shoulder also.

But I won the war and my garden thrived that year, but in the ensuing years I was somewhat reluctant to try it again. Two years later I capitulated and quit gardening.

THE GREAT OUTHOUSE RACE
BLACK FOREST, COLORADO-1972

In the annals of history it has been recorded that given the opportunity for free outrageous thought, comradeship and the opportunity to aid crippled children, a gathering of a few men will create the zaniest, craziest ideas imaginable. Especially when a few cold beers are thrown in. This occurred on May 10, 1972 at the Fox in the Forest Inn in Black Forest, Colorado. The result was the inception of The Great Outhouse Race, a distance of approximately 1 mile between the two taverns that existed in Black Forest, with all proceeds to go to the Special Olympics for Challenged Children.

The race was to be unique, a mad-dash competition featuring the areas finest err, almost-top-notch physical specimens, in the Mother of all Races. The proprietors of the two taverns, the Fox in the Forest and the Seahorse Bar, readily accepted the role of Grand Marshalls. The rules and regulations set forth by this august gathering were dutifully recorded on a roll of toilet paper for posterity.

Each entry was to consist of a sponsor, ten men (eight runners and two alternates) plus a female throne rider. The throne rider was to be helmeted and strapped in with a seat belt. Two prizes were to be awarded; one for speed and one to the sponsor who acquired the most donations. A special small commode would be provided to each sponsor for collecting these offerings. It was also agreed, that prior to notifying the local citizenry of the impending momentous event of which they would be a party thereto, all plans would be held secret until the special racing vehicles were built.

Local carpenters, who were bonded for two bucks, built the vehicles in absolute secrecy. A nearby lumberyard, with visions of unmatched advertising benefits via national television coverage a near certainty, donated the lumber. It must be noted that these benefactors had their names recorded in the bylaws for recognition or notoriety-whichever came first. Two sleek, identical custom-made aerodynamic vehicles were constructed containing a commode in a small wooden shed, mounted on two wooden beams fifteen feet in length. Handles for eight men were added. After construction the design plans were placed in a secure beer can and buried in a never-to-be-revealed location.

Thus the challenge went forth, to all local villages and towns, plus every bar therein, that a race was to be had for brave participants only. The gauntlet was down. The challenge was received at the Bella Vista Bar on North Nevada Street in Colorado Springs. Ken Wiedlick, my friend and neighbor, owned the bar. Ken was an affable, retired army sergeant who was the father of a mentally retarded daughter. He was also a gambler who liked to roll dice and was a regular patron at Las Vegas.

One story about Ken described the man. I was tending bar for Ken one night when he was in Vegas. Around 10 p.m. the phone rang, it was Ken. "Set up the bar he shouted, all drinks are free for the rest of the night. The dice are hot and I'm 25 grand ahead." The Bella Vista closed at 2 am so I realized I had a busy night ahead! Hell, the word about free drinks had filtered out, and people were flocking in. Then at 11:30 the phone rang, it was Ken shouting, "Make the freeloading bastards pay for their drinks, no more free tab, I'm down 5 grand." Easy come-easy go.

The Bella Vista was located about halfway between my residence and the Hewlett Packard facility on Garden of the Gods Road, where I was employed. I stopped there occasionally and seriously considered becoming a partner with Ken at the establishment. I was present when the challenge was received and immediately accepted. While Ken negotiated the entry rituals, a race team was assembled of which I was a member. The subject of training came up once, and it was agreed that a strong grip was vital. Thus a toast of beer glasses was raised, all in a firm grip. Dallas Hunter, a retired businessman from Philadelphia was present and immediately accepted the position of Treasurer. Dallas was a tall white haired gent, always nattily attired in a dark suit and tie, a jaunty figure who was at the ready with an appropriate quip. Dallas kept the quantity of collected donations a closely guarded secret for as he noted, "There are spies and thieves amongst us." He was a lover of poetry and the grape. Dallas and I had an annual wager of 25 cents on the football rivalry between Pennsylvania's titans of the gridiron; he had East Stroudsberg State and I had Slippery Rock. Dallas promptly dubbed the Bella Vista racing team as the "North Nevada Neurotics" and no one argued.

The race was a barnburner; everyone had a good time, even the two throne riders whose outhouse got dropped-thank God for seat belts. It was noted that their runners arrived very early and spent a lot of time sipping suds. The racing course was thronged with approximately 700 onlookers and ambulance drivers. There were 20 teams, and the winner was a team from the Air Force Academy. All the participants suspected foul play for the Academy cadets appeared to be in superb physical condition.

The accidents that occurred did not go unnoticed by our alert team. The next year, a member of our team obtained the first-ever insurance policy covering a throne rider in an Outhouse Race. The runner, an insurance agent, requested a policy from his home office in Lincoln, Nebraska and they, after determining he wasn't a certified nut, grabbed the spirit of the moment and proudly stated in it's newsletter " they had achieved a first in racing history."

Our team tied for the category of "those that lived through the race and didn't kill anyone." But Ken was vindicated when the collected donations were announced and Dallas boomed out $1505-the Bella Vista Bar is the winner!

SAGES OF INFORMATION
THE BARTENDER & THE BARBER

There is an old adage that proclaims, "In all towns across the United States exist two fountains of wisdom and information that echews all convention and can be readily tapped to obtain local lore, history or direction." No, it is not the local newspaper or library, the incredible source of knowledge resides with the barber or the bartender. These sage gentlemen are truly the repositories of incredible knowledge, humor and occasionally-rumor. No subject is too difficult or too small to be listed in his or her Pantheon of Tall Yarns. Little did I realize that one-day, I would lend credence and enhance their reputation.

It occurred in 1978, at the Erin Inn on North Academy Boulevard in Colorado Springs, Colorado. While working at Hewlett Packard as a design engineer, I had become a partner in the Inn with Leo Swanson, and on June 10, I was filling in for the regular bartender on a very slow evening. At 7 P M, two gentlemen entered the lounge, and after checking out the booth area, turned and entered the bar and sat down on the available stools. Upon seeing the two gents, I immediately recognized the company they represented. No, I wasn't psychic, and I didn't know them personally, but IBM reps stood out like a whore in church.

They were attired in the company mandated dark suit, with red tie and clean-shaven. During the1960s and 70s, Big Blue, as IBM was called, held their employee's total lifestyle in check. Facial hair was taboo, where an employee cashed his payroll check was monitored and if you drank-it better not be in the company owned country club, for "the word got around."

What'll you have, I asked? Two beers, draft came the reply. I began filling two steins but kept my ears glued to their conversation. There were only two other people at the bar and they weren't together so the place was very quiet. Even the jukebox was waiting for a slug.

I was right, the two men were IBM sales engineers and they were discussing an electrical circuit problem that they encountered at a nearby customer. I delivered the two beers and stayed close by. I recognized the problem they were discussing as one I had encountered from time to time. It was a common problem that test and measure-ment engineers had to anticipate when designing new measurement equipment.

I waited patiently, and inwardly smiled, while the two men intensely studied their problem. Soon they ordered two more beers, and I, after delivering the suds, paused over their diagram that they had sketched out on a bar napkin. Deliberately hesitant, I apologized for interrupt-ing their conversation, and point blank asked if they needed help in solving their dilemma. "It will make your evening much more pleasant without this monkey on your back," I said. "I know that after a tough day I like to enjoy a beer without thinking about work." During this brief discussion, not a word was asked nor volunteered concerning my qualifications.

I noticed a slight smile begin on the lips of both men at the corner of their mouths. "Sure," was their reply, as they smirked at the thought of this obvious smart-ass about to make a fool of him? I got another napkin, redrew the diagram adding some components and deleted others. "Now I'll solve your problem, but wait a minute," I replied- "actually, you've got two problems." The two IBM men were no longer smiling, instead a look of incredulity had slowly covered their faces and remained frozen there. "But no problem," I interjected, "just go into the dual mode on the scope, set the sweep speeds here and the probes there and Voila, you'll have both answers."

Quickly I turned but kept an amused eye on the gentlemen using the large mirror that encircled the bar area high on the ceiling. The conversation between the two IBM sales engineers ceased. I never did reveal to the two gentlemen my true profession or background, I left that tidbit of knowledge to their imagination. Quickly they finished their beers and departed. Amused, I chuckled to myself and visualized the two men sometime in the future telling a listener, "There's this bartender in Colorado Springs who..

The stories of the wisdom possessed by bartenders and barbers are endless. Once, in a small mining town near Pittsburgh, the story involved a local barber. My father arrived in the Unites States in 1921 from Czechoslovakia and relocated in the coal country of Western Pennsylvania. Over the years, he repeatedly told the story of a strange but tense confrontation that occurred often between two men who resided in the area. One was an obvious thug and gangster, while the other was one of several barbers who plied his trade in the area.

The gangster, whose name was Tony, was somewhat of a dandy. He always wore very expensive suits, and daily without exception, stopped for a trim and shave at one of the local barbershops. He also had one very unnerving trait, for upon entering any shop, he would pull out a revolver and warn the barber that should the barber "nick him" during the shave, the barber would be a dead man, right there. To emphasize his statement, Tony would place the revolver on his lap.

In a short period of time, Tony's antics spread throughout the region until all barbers but one refused his business. This one barber was also from Czechoslovakia and he and Dad conversed regularly in their native tongue whenever Dad visited the shop. Stefan, the Czech barber, had no compunction shaving Tony for he represented business, and the gangster was a very generous tipper.

One day the inevitable happened and curiosity was the instigator. Tony confronted Stefan, while getting a shave, with the obvious question. "Why is it that you're the only barber to accept my business, you don't even hesitate to shave me," asked Tony? "In fact you are the only barber in the area that will do it! Do you think you're perfect," snarled the gangster, "and never make mistakes?"

The question was asked while Stefan was shaving him with a freshly honed straight razor. Stefan paused for a second, smiled and never answered, but he gently tapped Tony's throat with the razor and continued the shave in long delicate strokes.

There was one other story that Stefan related to immigrants that arrived in the coal region and visited his Barbershop. His shop, like others in the area, was a center for information mainly because many languages and dialects were spoken there, and the clientele was male. This story concerned trust and money.

The coal miners in the Monongehela River region, near Uniontown, Pa., were predominately from the Eastern European Area. The men, well known for being hard workers, were predominately Czechs, Croats, Serbs, Yugoslavians, Poles and Hungarians. Most of these men could speak four or five different languages but English was not one of them.

It seems a crew of new immigrants was discussing money near the mine tipple prior to entry into the mine. They had just had their first payday and they didn't understand their pay. It wasn't money but instead a funny piece of paper that supposedly said they had money. This pay slip was new to them. A Forman, who overheard the conversation, and understood part of the dialect, as he and 99%

of management were of English descent, intervened and offered to help. The men, extremely leery, questioned him.

He explained that the slip could be turned into money at the local company store. In fact, he would do it for them. Reluctantly they agreed if one of the crew accompanied him. Naturally, the guy selected by the crew was Lech, a Pole and the biggest man in the group.

All went well and each man received his money. This transaction went on smoothly for several months, until one of the men compared his wages to his neighbor's who did the same job. His neighbor was taking home more money. Several members of the crew searched out older miners who had been there for years. Sure enough, something was amiss. Next payday, Lech was sick and couldn't accompany the Forman to cash the pay slips. In his place was an old-timer, a "cousin who knew the ropes." The Forman was suspicious but couldn't alter the money on the "spur of the moment."

The Forman distributed the money to the crew, nothing else was said. After the Forman left, the old-timer told the men that they were being cheated.

Stefan ended the story, but naturally everyone listening asked, "What happened?" All Stefan said was, "I've never been in a mine but all miners agree on one thing, coal mines are dark and dangerous, there are a lot of places were a serious accident can happen."

A LONG RIDE BACK
GREYHOUND BUS, DENVER TO ELMIRA, NY-
1978

The great American plains have posed an obstacle and a dilemma throughout the history of the early settlers and pioneers. They were an omen that required a decision by those in passage-now it was my turn. It was quiet in the bus, and the only audible sound was the Greyhound's motor as the miles passed by through my window. The featureless landscape offered no answers or promises. Occasionally I got a glimpse straight ahead, out the driver's window, hoping to see a change in the terrain, but to no avail as the forlorn, featureless flat land of eastern Colorado monotonously rolled on. I had passed this way before and knew the next hill wouldn't occur for another 700 miles, when we crossed the Mississippi. Traveling east from Denver on Interstate 70 is a disillusioning trek, a long flat ride through an unforgiving landscape.

The time was October 1978, the exact date didn't matter as time had lost its meaning and I had forever to make this trip. Thus, I had decided to travel via a slow, smelly bus, as I wanted time to think. The time for platitudes and alternatives were past; I knew what the immediate future held, but I was delaying the inevitable as long as possible. My destination was Elmira, New York-at least three days away. I could have flown; I had five grand in my pocket, but I wanted the long, slow way as time was not of the essence. One week later I will have proven my point.

It was a time for soul-searching, to remember some things and forget others; I was indeed at a crossroads. Currently I was unemployed, but not concerned, as I possessed talents that were much in demand. At present, I had an open job offer in Beaverton, Oregon as a Senior Engineer, thus employment was not a problem. My marriage was the major problem, plus I had a nagging concern about alcohol. For the last few years, the grape tasted too good; it was something I had to address.

This day I carried my memories with me in a brown paper bag. Thirteen years earlier I had traveled this same route as I drove from Chicago to Colorado Springs. Chicago had been a scene of success for my career, as it brought me recognition, money and unfortunately introduced me to the three-martini lunch.

Colorado had been a continuation of success, thirteen good years of contributions, but then I burned out. My psyche demanded a change and until I had a permanent solution I resigned from Hewlett-Packard and tried a new venture a co-owner of an eating and drinking establishment, the Erin Inn. The move was a miscalculation as the seeds of alcoholism fertilized and blossomed. The malady has a fiendish nature that often thrives during periods of success, then compounds its insidious nature by ravaging an individual during bouts of depression and desperation.

The Greyhound rolled on, miles passing by, just the droning of the engine to be heard and occasionally, the rustle of the brown paper bag. Stops were frequent, but I didn't get off, I had my refreshments with me, they were enveloped by a large package of memories.

I dissolved my partnership after two years, then after much contemplation decided to head east to Elmira in an attempt, albeit a very meager one, to rescue a marriage already beyond salvation. Many personal differences preceded the separation, and now it was difficult to distinguish the exact root cause, but one thing I had to confess, I was also a party to its failure. I quietly cursed myself for not seeking an amicable divorce much earlier, but now it was too late for what might-have-been.

Nightfall thankfully arrived and wrapped around the vehicle as the mileage increased, but thankfully it obscured the never changing scenery. I sat alone in the back of the half-empty bus, alone with a myriad of memories. Thinking of Elmira depressed me and then I thought that the trip should be slowed-perhaps I should stop somewhere and contemplate my actions, but where? Then I saw a road sign indicating the Kansas border was ahead, and I thought about an old Kristofferson song about Salinas. His Salinas was probably in California but the one in Kansas was my goal. The song extolled a guy named Bobby MaGee, a guy who slipped away at Salinas-maybe I could too. Either way it sounded like a nice place to pause, but I had a few hours to kill as Salina was almost in the center of the state, if my geography was correct. So I leaned back and took a few long swigs and closed my eyes.

I tried to sleep but couldn't, and then it dawned on me. This was my first trip when time was not a factor, hell- it wasn't even in the equation. It just didn't matter when I arrived at anywhere! I had no job, no schedule and no timetable. Deep down the feeling was pleasant and relaxing; I guess the vagabond, a long time resident, still existed in my soul. Jack Kerouac would have been proud. I spent the rest of the evening siting wide awake thinking that maybe it was time to just vanish, a feeling that was easy to understand and difficult to forget.

The bus rolled into Salinas at mid-morning the next day; I had forgotten what day it was. I kept thinking about my current situation, for I was alone in a strange town with no friends-but that situation never bothered me in the past, in fact I enjoyed it. To be alone in a strange place, better yet a foreign land brings forth the essence of character in a traveler, for now he discovers who he really is! In my prior wanderings I had been alone in Europe and also in Africa, so Kansas was a walk in the park.

I got off in Salinas and rebooked my ticket for a future undefined time- then walked outside to greet Kansas. It was a warm day, but the portent of winter lingered in the air. That was OK, as winter was less opaque to decision making. I noticed a tavern across the street from the bus depot and decided to enter and meet the local populace. Also, I learned a long time ago that a bartender is the best source of local information, except perhaps the resident barber. I spent the next two days amid thought-filled analysis and alcoholic oblivion, all the while bending the bartender's ear. The regulars also enjoyed my presence as I regularly set up the bar, for money was no object. Happy Hour lived up to it's name, and if I stayed much longer in Salinas I could have run for Mayor and won in a landslide. My nights were spent upstairs over the bar in one of the three available rooms for $12.00 per night.

Solutions for my problems were as rare as trees on the Kansas plains. I couldn't fathom as to how I permitted myself to arrive at this juncture. My wife and I had few common interests, and for sixteen years we ignored that fact while letting our unhappiness fester until the present situation resulted. Our attraction for each other had been strictly physical, and common sense was not a bed-partner. Now a decision based on reality was not only prudent but also damned necessary. Unfortunately our son Kevin would pay the price, but I knew I had to go to Elmira, her hometown, for the final chapter of the story. So after two days and three nights of conversation concerning grain, cattle, crops and the weather, I understood why I loved the mountains and the forests, as the flatlands held no interests or answers. Thus on the third evening I boarded the bus once again at 9 pm and headed east.

We arrived in the Windy City, and I again decided to postpone the inevitable and remained in Chicago for almost two days. It was two days of revelry, music and good times with old friends on Rush Street. The booze flowed, as it was my treat for old friends Bill and Ted, from the

Admiral Corporation, who joined me in these last hours of my journey. Then, once again, in the evening, I left and headed east to face the past, and hopefully begin a future.

The bus arrived in Williamsport, Pa. at 11:45 pm, fifty miles short of Elmira. I was then informed that it was the end of the line for that day and at 8 am the bus for Elmira would depart. My adrenaline was flowing at a fever pitch and remaining in Williamsport was totally unacceptable. It was a crisp cool autumn evening and I was attired in a Pendelton, Oregon wool overcoat and determined to reach Elmira, so I hired a cab to the route #15 north turnoff, and I hitch hiked to Elmira. I was very familiar with the area, as Penn State, my alma mater, was only 45 miles distance. I wanted a final closure to the entire episode.

My last ride into Elmira, at 4:30 am was on a milk truck. The driver, a very affable gent, not only drove me into Elmira but to my brother-in-laws doorstep. That earned the driver a very generous tip. Thus I arrived in Elmira some seven days and a bunch of hours after leaving Denver to dissolve my marriage. The "cheap" bus trip "only cost" approximately $2000 but I was not regretful, as years of frustration were removed, and I was on a course to begin a new life.

There was something magical about that trip, it was like a flying carpet ride. There were no enemies or troubles, only hardworking folk trying to get it all together, "to make it." Maybe Bobby MaGee and I were looking for the same El Dorado, a place we'd never find.

Quite often, as the years pass, I think back to that time, that trip, and two words come back to haunt me, like a recurring dream, "What If?"

A SINGLE, SOLITARY SUITCASE
FRANKFURT, GERMANY-JULY 9, 1987

Finally, after an unusually long wait-even for transatlantic flights, the Boeing 747 crept away from the loading gate and proceeded down the tarmac to enter a line of aircraft waiting for control tower permission to depart. Then suddenly a strange event occurred. The plane pulled out of the line and taxied to a secluded location on the taxi runway, stopped and all four engines were shut down. I was startled. I had made many flights, but to abort the taxi to the takeoff runway was a new experience.

Claire and I had just spent a week in Hannau visiting my son Kevin and his new bride. We had expected to witness the ceremony, but they decided to complete the nuptials before we arrived. Disappointed, but with all reservations finalized, we came anyway. During our visit we had very delightful side trips to Heidelberg and Zurich, Switzerland.

As we sat in the aircraft with the engines off, tension and anxieties began to mount among the passengers.

Whispers pertaining to terrorists and bombs began to emanate. Then hesitatingly, the pilot's voice came over the intercom and advised that "All was well, however, a minor incident concerning luggage had occurred and needed to be rectified. It was a procedural problem," he added.

The passengers clung to every word he uttered, and while his explanation induced a somewhat calming effect, anxiety abounded. Airline passengers are fully aware of the precarious and vulnerable position they occupy.

This was Claire's second trip to Europe, and stories concerning terrorists dominated the headlines. During our first trip in 1985, German police carrying automatic weapons forcibly removed a man of Arabic decent from our train car. Whether he was a criminal, we never learned, but it was an incident that unnerved many passengers. I believe that Claire enjoyed our trips to Europe, but I also suspect that she was nervous throughout and always gratified to see Boston again. Personally, I was sad the trips ended!

The pilot then issued another edict, "All passengers must descend the portable stairs brought to the aircraft by terminal personnel and stand on one side of the aircraft while all luggage is unloaded." Slowly, the aircraft was emptied and the luggage placed in a line on the tarmac. At that time each passenger was asked to identify their personal luggage which was immediately removed from the tarmac by airline personnel and reloaded aboard the plane. This exercise, concerning 300 passengers and their luggage, took several excruciating and irritable hours punctuated by curses (in many different languages), shouts and audible statements concerning terrorist plots.

Finally the plane was reloaded with passengers and luggage, the engines restarted and the plane slowly began to taxi when I saw "It". I was seated in a window seat on the side of the plane where the luggage had been placed for identification. Claire was next to me, as she didn't want an "outside view." There it sat. A brown, tattered, inconspicuous, unclaimed suitcase sitting alone on the tarmac. Why, why didn't someone claim it, whose suitcase was it, what was in it, could there be another one that was missed and suddenly that suitcase assumed immense proportions. I stared hard at the satchel, trying to peer inside, hoping for x-ray vision, but all I saw was leather bound questions. My mind conjured up countless apprehensions, very few of which were pleasant.

I immediately diverted Claire's attention, but I heard murmurs from ahead and behind-hushed whispers pertaining to "It". An eternity later our plane entered the take-off procession. Gradually we inched forward until it was our turn to depart. Under full power we roared down the runway and then, hesitatingly peering right, I got one last gut-wrenching glimpse of the suitcase far in the distance. Not wanting to unnerve Claire, I kept silent about the incident until we deplaned in Boston. Chatter about the episode diminished during the flight, as passengers tried vainly to forget. I never closed my eyes during the entire flight back, and every little bump was cause for concern. It kept coming back, was it accidentally left over from a previous flight, could it possibly be someone's dirty laundry, or was it a bomb?

When we landed, I grabbed several newspapers searching for an article concerning an incident at the Frankfort Airport but found none. But then I pondered; if I was in control of an airport that just narrowly averted a disaster, would I advertise it?

Many times over the years I reflect back to the incident and oft times it reminded me of another harrowing flight. It occurred on August 7, 1956 as I was aboard a C-121 Constellation flying from Tripoli, Libya to Fort Dix, New Jersey when the outboard engine, on my side, slowly stopped turning. We had passed Gibraltar and were over the eastern Atlantic at 20,000 feet, and the pilot had just informed the passengers that " we had passed the point of no return." I knew that the "Connie" was a very reliable aircraft and could fly with three engines, but that dead engine provided for a "white knuckle flight" for the rest of the journey.

A PAUSE FOR HISTORY
LES CHAMPS ELYSEES, PARIS-JULY 25, 1988

We sat there, Claire and I that warm July afternoon sequestered in time. We were alone amidst a sea of humanity on the sidewalk of History's City. Our vantagepoint was a small curbside table of an outdoor Café that permitted an unobstructed view of the spectacle that played out before us. However, I sensed an eerie feeling, for I was somewhat oblivious to the turmoil of activity that engulfed the scene. There were others present, not yet seen, who were vying for center stage.

Before us, the Champs Elysees stretched its tentacles, multiple lanes laden with autos, bicycles, tourists, gendarmes, bustling crowds- yet I continued in my reverie of a time long past and sensed the arrival of apparitions surfacing in my mind.

To our left stood the magnificent Arc de Triomphe, anchoring one end of the Champs Elysees in the Place de l'Etoile. It commemorates the glories of Napoleon I and was constructed during the time span of 1806-1836. The monument has endured regional conflicts, world wars and domestic rebellions, while looking down upon armies, victorious and vanquished, marching with helmet and beret through its portals. Its faÁade is adorned with sculptures depicting memorable battles while within lies the crypt of a fallen unknown warrior.

This day, the cacophony of marching feet was silent, except in the chambers of my mind. There I could hear and see them, ghosts marching with pale visages staring with haunting, unseeing eyes. They were in a parade of destiny marching to silenced drums but with a rhythmical cadence of pounding feet growing louder, as jackboot and brogan, stomped their presence in time. Then as quickly, silence returned as the phantoms passed in review.

The armies took their turn in silent tribute. Napoleon's victorious legions of the 1800's, followed by their conquerors of June 1815. Then the partisans of the 1852 and 1870 rebellions marched, trailed by the armies of 1918- the "War to End all Wars." Finally, the German conquerors of June 14, 1940 passed, followed by the Allied Army of August 25, 1944 that crushed the dreaded Wehrmacht. Each had their appointed time in the annuals.

Returning from the past I looked to my right as the boulevard of Time sloped downward, emptying the echoes of history on the deaf ears of Paris. In the distance I espied the soaring structure of the Eiffel Tower, its presence dominating the skyline as it had since 1889. More distant, the uppermost tops of the twin towers of the Cathedral of Notre Dame were faintly discernible. This remarkable edifice, built during the span of 1163-1330, has also resisted the ravages of a war-torn era.

Claire and I were very quiet, content with sharing the spectacle together, but in awe of History. Our table was small and covered with a red-checkered cloth that faintly revealed wine spots of other witnesses who drank in the scene before us. I sat there mesmerized, savoring every morsel of history to digest again at some future time.

The sun gradually became warmer as the afternoon slipped by, even though we sat in the shade of a large red parasol. Reverently, we sipped our wine knowing that on this day we drank a rare vintage whose grapes were crushed by feet not of our time and aged in the wooden casks of antiquity.

Paris, a city for the ages, whose architecture depicts the trials and tribulations of Man's History, celebrated its 2000th anniversary in 1951 and on this day lives on. Then I recalled a passage of literature that extolled, "If you sit by the side of the Champs Elysees long enough, sooner or later, every person in the world will eventually pass by." This day was the time for Claire and I.

CENTER STAGE
THE KRASNAPOLSKY HOTEL, AMSTERDAM-
1988

It has been said "that all the world is a stage" and everyone will be allotted their "fifteen minutes of fame" but only a chosen few are cognizant of the special occasion as it arises and seizes the golden opportunity. This evening was destined to be one of those rare occurrences when the Gods smiled on that fateful last night in Holland as Claire and I were about to depart for Boston at dawn. That night, a magical moment occurred. It was not earth shattering or mind boggling, but it captivated the two of us and we sat mesmerized as a special circumstance punctuated our last evening, as only lovers are destined to share.

We had arrived in Amsterdam by train from Paris and quickly settled in at the hotel. The trip, which had taken six hours, was unforgettable. We had traveled north through the peaceful French countryside, passed the quaint villages of Le Mons and San Quentin, while enjoying the luxury of a clean, punctual rail system. I often marveled at the United States, a great country that had demonstrated the technical ability to send several successful expeditions to the moon, leads the world in nuclear technology, and yet can't produce an efficient and timely mass transit system to equal those of Europe.

After checking in our hotel, we decided to explore Amsterdam by boat, which is very practical as a myriad of canals, crisscross the sprawling city. At the dock we boarded a glass-covered boat that held approximately 40 people and soon were navigating the canals of Amsterdam as the tour guide regaled us of the wonders of Amsterdam, those present and others of the past.

Afterward we meandered back to the hotel and the repast that we promised ourselves. We had previously agreed that each of us would order a meal that we never before had eaten to celebrate our final night in Europe. We entered the main dining room and were greeted by the Maitre D and an enticing atmosphere of aroma, which tantalized the senses. After being seated amid an ambiance of a soft piano and delicate color we were greeted by our waiter. He was a very amicable professional of approximately thirty with a debonair flair of one schooled in every nuance of the culinary arts. We immediately conveyed our dilemma concerning our last night and he immediately responded with several appetizing suggestions from which Claire selected rabbit and I chose Italian guinea fowl, and for our soup, it was ox-tail. The waiter left quickly but returned just as fast with a single red rose for Claire, a memento of our last evening in Europe.

As we enjoyed a glass of wine we observed our waiter serving an obvious mid-eastern couple several tables away. I had recognized one of the entrees he delivered to the table; it was Dover sole, a very delectable flat fish coveted by connoisseurs. Soon thereafter I sensed a hubbub emanating from the tables around where the Dover sole was being prepared for serving.

The waiter had seized his moment. As he started removing the bony skeleton of the fish, he sensed the attention of the nearby patrons. Immediately he assumed the verve of an artist at work. His actions became more subtle and deliberate and every movement of his bladed hand became a parry or thrust of a fencer. Now the entire dinning room was in awe of his performance, as the room slanted downward to where his command performance was being orchestrated. Claire and I were included.

Slowly and gently he separated the skeleton from the body of the fish. His goal and crowning achievement would be the removal of the entire skeleton intact, a fait accompli.

As he withdrew the skeleton, I felt myself leaning forward in anticipation, but also to offer some silent assistance to the maestro. In fact, the entire room had become silent aides participating in the delicate surgery and was glued with rapt attention. Finally the entire skeleton was withdrawn, with nary a bone broken or missing. Applause was instantaneous from all sides as the entire dinning room assemblage applauded the performance. The waiter raised the skeleton overhead in acknowledging the recognition and then bowed in gratitude. The performance was successful.

While dining on our meal, which was sumptuous, I couldn't help but reflect that brief moments in time, as we had just witnessed, are welcome respites from the humdrum of life that most of us share and are indeed special occasions. To share these events with a special person gives togetherness an entirely new dimension, one that is long remembered and savored.

THE LAST FISHING TRIP
LAKE OPEONGO-ONTARIO, CANADA-1994

There was something disparate about the Balint brothers that appeared to transcend normal family relationships. They led totally different lifestyles, had different occupations and the age factor was always there. Yet even apart, their reasoning-likes and dislikes- were amazingly similar. These observations became unequivocal during 1994 on a sojourn to Canada, by the three brothers, on an occasion I entitled as "The Last Fishing Trip."

The occurrence had taken four decades to come to fruition, forty years of "almost, maybe or next year." The occasion almost slipped away as five years later, Bob died in an accident. The trips to Lake Opeongo, located in the Algonquin Provincial Park, commenced in 1957 when George and I made the first trip. Subsequently, the trip became an annual excursion, and for forty years George orchestrated the yearly ritual but the cast varied. On many trips during the 1970's our Dad went along, as mom had died and he was alone. Bob and George related many stories of the wonderful times they enjoyed with Dad; times I never had the pleasure of knowing. Now at last, for the three of us, the time was at hand. The long awaited trek was underway with the intended cast, but inconceivable as it may seem, this was the first time that the three of us went together.

Many events precluded an earlier happening; marriages, divorces, address changes and countless other intervening occurrences but now it was underway. Bob was seventy-one years old, George sixty-five and I brought up the rear at a mere sixty, a trio of old codgers setting out on a long awaited trip in August 1994.

We now lived in divergent locations across the Eastern United States; George lived in Ohio, Bob in Pennsylvania and I in New Hampshire. George was the driver for the trip and after picking up Bob, swung by Nashua and then we three brothers headed due North for Ontario at 7:00 a m on August 12th, 1994. Prior to entering Quebec however, we paused to share a libation and toast the journey. Traversing the Province of Quebec, we eventually passed Ottawa and drove on to the Provincial Park arriving at 11:00 pm. The late arrival prompted us to select the first campsite available, as the evening was only a brief respite. The next day required traveling, via canoe, traversing Lake Opeongo.

Early August provides a celestial bonanza for sky watchers, as the Perseids meteor shower puts on a dazzling display, so immediately after erecting our tent we walked to lakeside to observe the performance.

The Perseids did not disappoint us that evening but George and I had a hearty laugh as most of the spectacular meteors flashed behind Bob's back. He just wasn't fast enough to turn in time but his reasoning was we took the "best seats."

Our trip North the next day was eagerly anticipated, finally, three brothers were close to the destination. Our canoe was laden with gear and I sat precariously on top in the center of the craft. We made one stop on the way to Windy Point, our destination. All of us, at one point in time, had camped at the location which was a promontory jutting out into the lake. Our stop was a brief one, a celebratory pause to "drink to the occasion." Thus Bob raised the bottle of Crown Royal and we each had a swig, or as George put it, "a Wee Deoch and Doris" which is a Scottish toast that means, "a small drink before I go." George had picked up the salutation while golfing at St. Andrews.

After several hours, we reached our destination-Windy Point. The name for the site was ours and it is not cited on any map but it is very appropriate as a breeze is constantly in motion.

At Windy Point, George and I immediately erected the tent as Bob exercised his favorite chore, collecting and cutting firewood. That night, as we lay back in our tent, the call of the wild wafted through-the cry of the loon. It reminded me of another denizen of the wild who possesses a mournful cry-the coyote. Many times in the Rockies, at the same point in the day, I had listened to its soulful cry.

The second day we decided to return to the previous day's embarkation site, and obtain more food supplies, as our full load to the campsite, precluded our bringing a sufficient amount. I was very uneasy on the trip down the lake as the previous day's venture was very unstable but I kept silent. I should have voiced my concerns and regretted it. Again, I was perched high in the center of the canoe, watching the whitecaps cover the lake as a wind had arisen, when it happened. We were two-thirds across the lake, and in a split second, all three of us were in the water.

I came up directly under the canoe and, after banging my head twice, it occurred to me that I should try a different tact. I grasped the two sides of the canoe, then rolled to my right and voila, fresh air. Bob and I were on the same side of the canoe but George wasn't in sight. Twice I called his name but received no reply. Then we heard coughing and a sputtering reply, he was okay but had to dispel some excess water. We all were good swimmers and there was no panic or reason for alarm. Luckily, the capsizing didn't occur the day before when the canoe was laden with our camping gear but we did incur some losses. My Minolta 35mm camera was ruined and Bob's eyeglasses went to the bottom of Lake Opeongo. The glasses proved once again the similarity of the brothers. As soon as we hit shore I passed my glasses to Bob, as I only used them when reading, and bingo-almost a perfect fit.

The shoreline was a long way off and as we discussed our predicament, a single canoe rounded the bend and in it was a lone occupant, a teenage girl. She passed us a rope, while not getting too close as her obvious training had taught her, and then slowly towed us to the shore.

The incident awakened us to reality, we weren't kids anymore and the accident was a possible omen to "take it easy." Thus, we then changed our plans and after retrieving our gear from Windy Point, with the help of the Ranger's powerboat, we set off and established a camp at a nearby campground.

The rest of the week was spent appreciating the camaraderie and long discussions concerning oft-pondered questions concerning our parents, relatives, religions, politics, and literature-especially poetry-were held deep into the night. The camaraderie was unforgettable; it had taken far too many years and now we asked and dissected with zest, the many intriguing queries that had haunted us for years. It was astounding that our thoughts, reasoning and rationalizations were amazingly similar.

Virtually every evening remained the same and it was obvious that each of us relished, with anticipation, the banter and topics that lie ahead. This was true even though a lot was a rehash of the previous evening's agenda. Hurriedly, we ate our dinner and collected firewood for the evening. The dinner plates were paper so their disposal was the campfire. Then the strategic placement of the iced cooler took place, close to the fireside but within everyone's reach, for an occasional libation. After locating a log or some other comfortable seat a silence of anticipation, along with the shades of nightfall, descended on the camp. Continued silence permeated the night as three intellects shared private thoughts and reverie.

I had difficulty believing my ears, was it possible? We had traveled different paths, chose radically different lifestyles and yet, as the campfire chats continued, it was as if we never left home. Those fireside chats shall forever occupy the reserved chambers of my mind. They were unique.

It was poetry however, that captivated most of our conversations. The primary subjects of our discussion were Shakespeare, Coleridge and Thomas Gray. Bob's favorite was the sonnet "Polonius' advice to Laertes" from Hamlet, while George and I drifted to Gray's "Elegy in a Country Curchyard." But we all came together with Coleridge's "Rhyme of the Ancient Mariner." Occasionally I produced an old poetry book that I've carried for many a year to review a line or stanza of note. There, under the stars we spent hours remembering various lines and diagnosed them long into the night, as the fire burned low. Gradually, while deep in thought and the wee morning hours approaching, the conversations slowed and then silence reigned supreme but still we lingered knowing full well that these gatherings were also coming to an end. We each edged closer to the fire but silence remained as the private personal curtains of reverie opened. I glanced at Bob and then George. They were not consciously present as they were buried in times past.

Bob initially drew my attention as his physical movements had slowed in recent years revealing his age. That night, looking at him, I recalled a few of his past endeavors as he rarely spoke of his past. Bob had defied the Grim Reaper on several occasions. In Jacksonville, Fla. while in flight school, sickness kept him grounded one day-a day his plane crashed. Then in the South Pacific, flying a dive-bomber from the carrier Intrepid against the Japanese, he was shot down twice and crash landed in the ocean. Remarkably, the same destroyer picked him up both times. Upon discharge, against the advice of everyone, he returned to the coal mines as an electrical foreman. Again, he survived an explosion within the mine and later retired. He was divorced from his first wife and his second died of heart complications. Five years later, in 1999, Bob tripped and fell down the steps at the old homestead late one night and died from the injuries.

Slowly I turned from Bob and viewed George. If Bob was an enigma, George was a conundrum within an enigma. After being discharged from the Army Air Corps, George returned to Masontown for several years and then moved to Cleveland, Ohio where General Motors employed him for 35 years. George never married and while employed at GM, attended Western Reserve University and the Case Institute of Technology at nights. He always had a keen analytical scientific mind and majored in Metallurgy that became his career at GM. His prowess and contributions were apparent at GM and he received an invitation from MIT in Cambridge, MA to give a seminar on his techniques of analyses involving Stainless Steel. Naturally, being George and true to his personality and demeanor, he declined the invitation from the prestigious institution. It was a chance moment, at the Masontown VFW in 2001, after a few beers that I learned of his technical reputation. Many other kudos have obviously been tossed his way, of that I'm certain, but they will remain unknown.

Very reluctantly we entered the tent at the end of the day. Soon, it was time to leave Canada and head south. It had been an assemblage of brothers long to remember and difficult to leave.

For the record, let it be known that during the entire trip, not one fish was caught and nobody cared! But scattered on nature's carpet of pine needles resided the shards of man's finest literature never to be more appreciated.

THE HALE-BOPP COMET
WITNESSED ON APRIL28, 1997
CLIFF HOUSE—OGUNQUIT, MAINE

It was a most singular event, awe inspiring and portentous. An unforgettable occurrence when words, and existence, pale to insignificance by the sheer wonderment that unfolded before us. High in the Northern Sky, enveloped by the darkened abyss of space, appeared a solitary traveler racing on a fiery orbit to a far-off rendez vous with oblivion.

Claire and I had selected the weekend to enjoy a romantic getaway at the Cliff House Resort in Ogunquit, Maine. The idyllic setting had been originally located by Claire, through a friend's referral, and now had become a frequent favorite retreat. As usual, the evening was memorable as we dined on baked stuffed lobster, abetted by a libation of Beaujolais, served in the Cliff House dinning room. There, amidst the culinary splendor, we toasted the evening's perfection while the vast North Atlantic expanse served as our stage.

Afterward, we strolled the grounds when suddenly we espied the visitor, and the evening became ransomed forever by the unexpected apparition. The Cliff House is a scenic arena of beauty, but this night, it became a footnote to history by the presence of a Silent Voyager in the Northern Sky.

On it traveled, an Omen-Spirit, trailing Comet's hair, scorching a cicatrix in the heavens as it plied its solitary journey, driven by phantom gods and subject not to a private destiny. Its final demise preordained by the Universal Laws of Physics. Mathematicians may have plotted its course, but it alone must make the journey.

Then suddenly, the forlorn object became familiar, as I realized I was actually peering into the very bowels of my being. It revealed the very essence of my existence for I too travel mostly alone to a predestined finality. Thus, we are but fellow travelers on a parallel course and our kismet a fait accompli.

Fare-thee-well my fellow traveler. Would that I could accompany your journey, a companion traveler, to witness your solitary trek that sketches a path of the last God going home to a final desire.

CONVERSATION WITH A NRA ADVOCATE
NATRONA HEIGHTS, PA. JUNE 1999

I say Sir, "It is time to visit the Constitution, especially the second amendment, for it is not prudent to have citizens walking the streets armed with automatic weapons." You state correctly that the amendment stipulates that "citizens have the right to bear arms," but you further state that you "will never relinquish that right and will always adhere to that position."

Now Sir, we have two problems. First and foremost, any further conversation on the subject is senseless. By your position and choice of the dogmatic words "never" and "always," you have revealed a mindset that is irreparably closed to dialogue or debate. You have shut your mind and sealed it against reasonable discourse or argumentation, thus you are incapable of enunciating sound judgment. I am among the first to defend our freedoms from the mindless bureaucracy known as government, but I am receptive to reason and debate. You, Sir, have reached

the position called Zealotry that precludes sound judgment or ability to debate.

Secondly, the constitutional authors created this marvelous document prior to the existence of the atrocious
methods of self-annihilation we now possess, or the mass
communication technology that potentially possesses the
destruction of man's greatest asset-individuality. From the
individual to the human race, our kismet is in our hands.
Thus we must proceed prudently and with great wisdom
before taking bold actions. Surely, those men of reason
contemplated future modifications would be required after hundreds of years, but you say "NO". In your eyes,
and those of your ilk, the document is sacrosanct-because
it fulfills your needs as written. I must proclaim that it is
marvelous, that you have elevated the authors to the sta-
tus of Gods, and thus we mere mortals are incapable of
questioning their work.

I say it is time to protect us, from ourselves. Thereby lies
the difficulty. For to add meaningful additions or modifications to the Constitution requires men of vision, and
today's society banishes that breed to question alone in
distant enclaves. It is a sad commentary on our current
generation but today's majority has a sinister entity, which
through chicanery and/or self-indulgence permeates our
society seeking only self- gratification.

Change, therefore, must be attempted for the benefit of
all citizens and it will be difficult to obtain agreement, for
profound insight is mandatory. But try we must, or the
Grand Democratic Experiment will fade into history, as

many of its predecessors have. Thus, with trepidation and with open minds, let us commence.

ARE THEY STILL VIABLE?
WILTON, NEW HAMPSHIRE-2001

With the advent of international terrorism to America's heartland on September 11th, certain fundamental questions have arisen pertaining to the intent and significance of the Constitution as written. A vast majority will immediately raise the flag and proclaim the amendments are sacrosanct; perhaps they are justifiably correct. But the question remains are we ignoring the inevitable? Are the freedoms we enjoy in America too potent an elixir for its citizens to drink? Those sacred proclamations demand respect and require constant vigil to protect them from those possessed with false ideals.

The unthinkable may have occurred, "are they incompatible with our current citizenry, or is it this Age of Technology and the world it has wrought?" Sadly, it may be both. Columbine initiated a nefarious trend of self-slaughter in America, and it is increasing with deadly frequency. Now, the September 11th disaster has overwhelmed all previous cataclysmic internal events in sheer magnitude, thus we must question certain aspects of the constitution, not for their flaws, but to equate their intent against the New World Order. International treaties and commerce, plus the relaxation of emigration requirements, bring added emphasis to the foundations of our democracy. Those tenets of our constitution, which govern inhabitants of this country and foreign visitors alike, must be understood and obeyed.

The September 11th debacle was perpetrated on the American homeland and against a population unforgivably unprepared. The threats had been previously made, and the end result was preventable, but again "at dawn we slept." One has only to observe the lifestyle of the current generation and the resulting ignorance that has trampled the Constitution. We have bent every amendment to permit the lavish and permissible activities that exist today. In addition, we have left open our doors for anyone to enter without paying their dues, and they also request equality. The September 11th incident illustrates that vicious intruders are taking advantage of our largesse and are entering the country, armed with hatred and jealousy and with firm resolve to destroy, kill and maim. The realization has become apparent; the moral fiber of America is being tested to determine if tenacity and resolve still exist, for this generation is inexperienced in economic and social hardships.

The First Amendment, which proclaims Freedom of Speech, was an acceptable institution until approximately 1960, but recently has been brutalized as newspapers and television sensationalize sex and violence, and contemporary music openly advocates crime and rape, in addition to the corruption of our language. Armed clans of militants, espousing hatred and racism, prowl our hinterland while citing the amendment to rally around.

The Second Amendment, the Right to Bear Arms, has placed weapons in the hands of the mentally incompetent, felons, mass murderers and children. From Columbine to this day, hardly a week passes without another atrocity occurring.

The Fourth Amendment, Search and Seizure, has become the felon's "Bill of Rights," as it has become the bastion of Drug Barons and Dope Dealers as they plead harassment while corrupting the youth of America. Meanwhile, assault on the Constitution's intent continues, aided and abetted by silver-tongued barristers whose sole interest is not justice but avarice.

But the real crime continues, as citizens demand "their right," with no desire to alter their lifestyle, and continue the flagrant abuse of those measures we hold so dear. Everyone who ever flew out of Boston knew that security was a farce, but it agreed with his or her "pell-mell" style of living. Thus the FAA and the Airlines will beef up security-for a while. But soon impatient customers will complain and "poof"- everything will revert back to "normal." Isn't it strange that El Al, despite operating in the Mideast, avoids aircraft highjacking?

The world has grown smaller, national boundaries have become mere lines in the sand, global enterprise has enveloped continents to the extent that those policies lionized 200 years ago require new thought and debate. "Arise America," it is not treason that we foster, but a search for the continuation of ideals and liberty. For freedom, in any language, is a harbinger of hope.

"Times, they are a changing," wrote Bob Dylan. It was a prophetic statement, but now we need not prophets or soothsayers, but leaders with the wisdom and foresight to take the Constitution and examine its compatibility with tomorrow's needs.

WANDERLUST
MASONTOWN, PA. -MARCH 20, 2000

It was an extraordinary feeling of deja-vu, which occurred during a period of surreal tranquillity. The time was 6 am and I was sitting alone in the basement of the old house at 124 Harbison Street.

There, in the eerie silence of the early morning gloom, I sat and quietly viewed my surroundings. I had risen early, and not wishing to disturb brother George, descended to the basement to collect my thoughts for the new day. Early wisps of daylight tried vainly to penetrate the last vestiges of night shadow. They, like the shadows in my mind, stubbornly remained. Silence reigned supreme in the dank, dusty cellar as I viewed the room. Everything remained in its place, the same as when I left-50 years ago-incredible! The old coal bin, the shower, the household appliances and on bookshelves-the same tomes as I remembered them. Briefly, I imagined I caught a glimpse of the old Bards: Shakespeare, Haggard, Chekhov, Ibsen, Tolstoy or perhaps Dostoevsky.

Did I ever leave? What happened to those 50 years, that half of a century? Did I really fulfill my childhood dreams and travel the world? If not, why do those names crowd my memory: Morocco, Sabratha, the Azores, the Gates of Hercules, Cape Canaveral, Eindhoven, Leige, High Lonesome, Pamplona-why are they there? Did I really go there, did I walk, talk and sleep there, or are they still a will-of-the-wisp-hoped for dreams that exist only in my mind! Or perhaps 50 years has not elapsed-but why is my hair gray and my hands wrinkled?

Haltingly, I looked around. The silence was deafening. Am I dead, I wondered? Is this shrouded melancholy my crypt? I'm afraid to try to stand, maybe I can't. I could attempt to speak, but what if no sound is there? Time passes slowly, there is no clock in view—there never was. I remain alert, straining my senses for a sound, but there is none. I notice that the gray wisps of dawn are winning their battle around me, but still, nothing stirs. If only a spider would venture by, some small indication of life, but nothing moves-everything is motionless.

Is this closure for me, or am I caught in a time warp, a kismet where I can view but not touch? But why, what significance would that entail? Perhaps I've been granted a reprieve, an opportunity to remain at home, to never leave and observe the effect on family and friends. Did my departure create misgivings of which I was never aware? But again I ask why, there are no guarantees that events would have been altered for the better. Was my presence necessary and were the family chains of love meant to enslave me from my wanderings?

I think not, destiny would still have been played out with the same cards. The urge to travel is difficult to understand unless you have been smitten by the pangs of the wanderlust. I say it is easier to ask a waterfowl to alter its course, to stop a wave in mid-ocean, or ask a moonbeam to stop halfway. My wanderlust has always been an insatiable desire to plant my footsteps where they have never been before, to walk on foreign shores amid strangers, and to observe events and cultures that were different. Danger is never a consideration, for a true traveler is armed with his greatest asset-self reliance.

I shall never truly know what hardships I created or left behind, perhaps even heartrending desires to keep me close. I only know where the North Star is and the touch of the wind at my back.

Were my actions understood? I doubt it, for to do so, one must savor the rhythm of the "Vagabond's Song". It's a timeless, discordant melody that only dreamers hear and dance to. A gypsy rhapsody that makes one drift and roam to the ends of the earth, as in a vagrants dream. Perhaps an answer exists in some far distant galaxy, but I'll have to go there to find it. I guess the quest never ends. It's just some eternal, remote thing that ranges across my imaginings.

Now I will try to rise and face reality.

A CHANCE ENCOUNTER
January 2001

It occurred in an instant, then vanished; white plumage against a snow-filled scene, a snowy owl was adrift in the forests of New Hampshire. The ghostly apparition existed for about 5 seconds. It rose on 6-foot wings from the woods on my right, crossed the road in front of me then faded into the snowy forest on my left. An alien from a strange, distant land, here... but for a visit.

Apparently the winter of 2001 was too harsh in the arctic tundra and, food being scarce, the raptor had ventured southward for a better clime. The snow-white plumage, absent of numerous dark bars, readily identified the bird as a male of the species. His nocturnal habits having gone awry in the far north, he now ventured forth during the twilight of this wintry day in New Hampshire. Thus, chance and fate spliced us together but for a brief moment.

It was 4 PM when the chance encounter occurred. I had left work at Kimball Physics Inc., and taking the long way home to Eastview Drive, I was traveling northeast on Route 45 towards route 101. I often took this leisurely route after work, as a time for relaxation and reflection, after a thought-filled day. Today I received a bonus, seeing the Visitor from the North. I know that I will take this route many times in the future, looking right and left for another glimpse, but it will not occur. I had been granted one memorable glance, and our paths shall never cross again.

A snowy owl is a silent predator, greatly feared by small birds, small animals and rodents. Unlike hawks and other raptors, owls possess feathers down to the talons, which muffles any sound that may occur, as the owl swoops down upon its prey. This silent approach, coupled with its nocturnal feeding habits, greatly enhance its menacing presence.

My mind flashed back to the winter of 1950. It was a very frigid, snowy winter; the most severe in my memory. The Monongahela River had frozen over and snows lay deep in the forest. The river is large, even by American standards. It is approximately 125 yards in width and 20-30 feet in depth as it meanders due North from West Virginia into Pennsylvania's bituminous coal fields to provide a water highway for steam driven paddlewheelers. The width and depth was necessary for the steamboats to maneuver the large laden coal barges up the river to feed the blazing steel furnaces in Pittsburgh. That year however, even the large sternwheeler icebreakers couldn't keep the river open.

I had been tending my trap line about a half mile down stream from Lardens' Bridge, on Route 21, near Masontown, Pa, and was engrossed in spotting any movement, on the ground, near my traps. The area was rife with fox and ermine and I was confidant to snare one, when swoosh, a large form flew low overhead. I had espied my first Snowy Owl. I was startled at the alien white form skulking among the trees. The sight left me awestruck, and long afterwards I had difficulty describing the vision to family or friends. It was his silent presence that unnerved me on that cold December day. Since I often frequented the area, I saw the silent predator on several occasions that winter, but never again did I enjoy the sight until 51 years later, at the chance encounter, in New Hampshire.

A TRAIL OF CARDS
MISSILE-SPACE FLIGHT INVOLVEMENT
1944-2001

My association with missiles, rockets and space flight was an apparent destiny, fulfilled. An incredible series of events that has spanned 57 years and today is racing to a final conclusion. A lifetime interwoven with a thread of circumstances that continually defined an apparent pre-ordained conclusion. Many times the path appeared to end only to resume at some distant location. Now I look back at the amazing sequence and marvel at the hand that fate dealt to me.

As a ten-year-old boy in Ronco, Pennsylvania in 1944, amid the poverty of Pennsylvania's coalfields, I built my first rocket. It was a very modest attempt that barely crept aloft, but portended dreams of visions untold. That initial missile, consisting of a solid propellant constructed from my chemistry set, spawned aspirations that dwelt among the stars.

In 1953 at Sampson AFB in upstate New York, after being bitterly disappointed by being rejected for Pilot's Training School, due to a temporary childhood speech impediment (stuttering), I was selected to attend a new ambitious training program in Newark, NJ. It was an accelerated course in organic chemistry to develop fuel analysts for America's burgeoning missile programs. Only two classes were ever to complete the program, mine was the last. The military deemed it more prudent to hire college graduates and for once, I agreed with them.

In 1956, the fateful day arrived, my fait accompli. I stood at the launch pad at Cape Canaveral, Florida. In front of me, poised for flight, was a gigantic Explorer Rocket, nose aimed skyward, a portent of the future. I was a fuel analyst for the United States Space Program. I had traded my boyhood's solid propellant mixture of blackpowder chemicals for the exotic liquid fuels that powered NASA's rockets into space. These liquid propellants, consisting of liquid oxygen, fuming sulfuric acid, 96% hydrogen peroxide and UDMH (unsymmetrical de-methyl hydrazine) were extremely volatile and dangerous to handle.

I had completed my analyses for the launch, all fuels were satisfactory, and all systems were "go". In approximately 12 hours, the missile will have been fueled and at 10 p.m., the fireball will rise to the heavens until its exhaust becomes a pinpoint among the stars.

Similar to events in Ronco, I witnessed many failures and missile explosions on the launch pad, but as in the infancy of many significant programs, knowledge crept out of every failure.

Finally my enlistment period ended and I was discharged from the Air Force in 1957. I was elated, yet saddened as I departed the Cape for a cloudy insecure future, leaving the Space Program behind. Little did I realize that missiles and space flight would always occupy my future. The cards were being dealt. Upon completion of my schooling at Penn State, my first job in private industry was at the Westinghouse Tube Division at Elmira, NY. In 1961, I signed on as a development and applications engineer for the F-4 Phantom Avionics System. I was involved with the guidance control displays for the Sidewinder Heat Seeking Missile.

In 1964, I left the defense industry and spent 18 successful years in the commercial segment of industry. My involvement included the television industry, test and measurement instrumentation and the microwave spectrum. Then, in 1982, at North Smithfield, RI, fate again intervened. The Amperex Microwave facility, at which I held the Manufacturing Manager's position, was sold and ceased to exist. Seeking a job, I was recruited by Raytheon and accepted a position as Senior Manufacturing Engineer for the Hawk and Seasparrow Missile Defense Systems. Once again, missiles were my total agenda.

In 1986, after a very successful performance, I was promoted to Senior Manufacturing Engineer for the Patriot Missile System. The $2 Billion dollar program was the largest weapons contract ever awarded.

Finally, in 1989, I retired from Raytheon. My missile days were over as I proceeded with minor contracting jobs in the private sector. Then fate played her Trump Card in

Wilton, NH. It was there, at 14 Eastview Drive, that Claire and I purchased our first home, a townhouse, on June 30, 2000. One day, in perusing the Nashua Telegraph employment section, an article jumped out at me. A Company, Kimball Physics Inc., was involved in Ion and Electron Gun Optics and was located in Wilton. My curiosity piqued. I called the company and arranged for an interview with Dr. Chuck Crawford, president and owner. I knew that if electron and ion guns were involved, the possibility of research and development with NASA loomed. After several discussions with Dr. Crawford I agreed to part time employment, 2 days a week, as a technical advisor.

Thus, as I pen this article, once again I recall ghosts of the past and dreams fulfilled. But now the trail has become more difficult and it is time for those more capable then I to enter the game. I'll just play out the hand that I hold.

DREAMS

They define tomorrow
Close the door on today,
Raise one's hopes to forever
And they'll never go away.

What purpose is life
If they vanish and disappear,
Tomorrow would be hollow
And today, insincere.

One can always question
Ponder and ask why,
But dreams all encompass
And, leave a spark, to try.

F.A. Balint

EPILOGUE
JOURNEY'S END-200?

He now walks with a shuffle, head slightly tilted, eyes partially glazed over with a far off look. Oftentimes he appears to be reading the future, which few dare to view, while smiling at the past. This old man's race has been run and shards of bygone exploits litter the wayside. Time-pieces and calendars are relics of the past, and the cadence in his shuffle has been replaced with a cane.

Plied with thoughts and memories, he plods along, his back bent with past deeds and time. His successes are long past and his failures too solidified to alter. Few recognize him in passing, and he is fully cognizant that soon his footprints will fade into oblivion. He has witnessed history, success and calamity; personal loss and personal gain now litter the roadside. Births have occurred, and good friends have opted to go quietly into that good night. He constantly ponders the consequences of his passage and acknowledges his era is closing, but he peacefully awaits the final curtain, as the death knell bodes little trepidation. He was fully aware that it was a one way trip and never desired a repeat performance, for he long ago acknowledged that he indeed was fortunate the first time and didn't dare tempt the Gods again. He was also forewarned that the further he traveled, the fewer friends would be present at the journey's end, but to him, it mattered not. He looks back not with sadness but with satisfaction.

Who is this old man? From whence did he come to walk the path he has chosen? What signposts, if any, guided him? Alas, there were few, but the untrodden pathway he chose had more appeal. His brow reveals few scowls but reflection and occasionally, traces of satisfaction, fleetingly appear. His only tinge of regret is, perhaps, he didn't go far enough, perhaps over that next hill and then......

His path traversed the far corners of the United States, sojourned to Europe and left footprints in the sands of Africa, always searching. Education and travel were his dossier, and science was the means. He argued the universe, politics, law and religion with scientists, politicians and charlatans as each had their brief moments on stage.

As with all participants in the great human drama, he is mystified by the swiftness of the play. He smiles at those who are always in a hurry to get somewhere or to complete some endeavor and asks why? Because our society demands it; "Damn Society," he replies! He chose to ignore tradition and the rest of society's foibles; he read his books, traveled his pathways and above all—indulged in self-education. He sought original thoughts and ideas and chose to ignore the current media conviction and dialogue. For early childhood taught him that education was the great Equalizer, and it prepared one for adversity. Education can be obtained in many ways but he chose travel and reading, especially classical literature, biographies and autobiographies. He developed his philosophy; do the unusual, ignore convention, select your own path and follow it. The earth is getting smaller, but untrodden byways still exist, and the aura of a successful venture is still captivating.

Then along the journey he found a friend, a companion and lover; a wonderful redheaded gal who enjoyed the walk with him and share the trek through life. Together they romanced in Newport and Galilee, engaging in sleeping on the beach and being awakened by the bells of lobster boats setting sail in the foggy mornings. Even once being awakened by a landowner who offered a cheery "Good Morning," while positioning signs on both sides of their sleeping bag proclaiming "No Trespassing."

They later married in Woonsocket, much to the chagrin of virtually every friend, as the 23-year age difference proclaimed a portent of disaster. The passing years however, proved the pundit's dire predictions totally unfounded. They honeymooned in New Orleans and eventually toured the United States and Canada. In subsequent years, their travels included Europe, visiting the Cathedrals of Cologne and Notre Dame, toured the canals of Amsterdam and savored the chocolate of Zurich. They dined at sidewalk cafes in Paris and climbed the Eiffel Tower. The world was their stage until they bought their home in Wilton, NH. Then it was the quiet solace of togetherness that captivated their existence.

During the journey he authored books, short stories, technical papers, manuals plus his beloved poetry. Copyrights and patents bear his signature but now the pen is going dry and the words more hazy within a cluttered mind. The bare page stares back, beckoning for words that flit in obscurity, as he reminisces of times and events that once were.

Lately an insidious malady, Parkinson's Disease, has slowed all physical activity, but the mental process is untouched. By his reasoning the price is fair; 67 years of good health-not even a broken bone- and now the Piper makes his call for payment due.

On he walks with a step slower still; how much further he knows not, but he will miss the redheaded gal! His desires have been fulfilled, and now he wishes that she also would savor a full cup of wine!

F. A. Balint

About the Author

From the coal dust laden streets of Ronco, Pennsylvania to the Champs Elysees, these stories reveal the soul of a man in search of himself. The journey crossed three continents and spanned half a century. This is my story and today, fifty years later, I find myself nestled with my wife Claire in the small town of Wilton, NH near the end of a satisfying journey.

I was born in Ronco and it was there that I developed an insatiable urge to learn and to travel. After acquiring a degree at Penn State, I commenced my odyssey.

It has been an electrifying experience and now I savor an elixir of quiet satisfaction

Printed in the United States
21562LVS00002B/340-399